I Am Here:
The Untold Stories of Everyday People

StoryShelter Presents

I Am Here:
The Untold Stories of Everyday People

Compiled by

Kerri Lowe & Melisa Singh

DEDICATION

This book is dedicated to the memory of
Michael Peppard and all of our loved ones who have
passed away with too many stories untold.

Carpe Diem

CONTENTS

Hidden Passions

Beating the Odds

Adventures

Overcoming Obstacles

Pivotal Moments

Everyday Heroes

Moments of Gratitude

Road to Knowledge

Family Ties

Forward

After taking an unexpected leap and leaving a job I found unfulfilling just a few days before the clock struck 2014, I was determinedly searching for my next move. When I saw the job description for a new website called StoryShelter, I had a good feeling. I don't think I can recommend leaving your job with no safety net, but I can say that for me, in this case, it worked out.

My personal journey had led me to a place where I recognized the power of telling our stories to help us heal and connect with one another. I realized that this wasn't just necessary for the artists and professional writers – everyone could benefit from telling their own story. This got me excited to be a part of StoryShelter.

My first inclination towards storytelling was in the theatre. I swore that someday I would be on Broadway, not tap-dancing in a musical, but starring in a dramatic play that would have the audience weeping in their seats. I moved to New York City to pursue acting in 2008 and instead found that my true form of expression was songwriting. I began writing country and folk songs about love, family and leaving home.

Pretty soon my plans changed to become a traveling singer/songwriter and release an album. Unfortunately a confluence of factors caused me to lose my voice. I couldn't sing without pain for two years and I had to realign my entire life. Losing my voice sent me on a journey of chronicling my past to understand where I had been and how I got here, teaching me about myself and how I might heal.

Telling the truth about my experiences through storytelling and making art are the only ways I know how to cope with setbacks, challenges and the pain of being human. Of course, it's also a great way to share joys and laughter (as you'll see from other stories in this book!) When we read the unfiltered stories of others we see ourselves in their words, growing our compassion and understanding of our own feelings and experiences.

The brave souls featured in this book are not keeping any secrets. From their most embarrassing mishaps to true hardship and turning points in their lives, the writers you are about to engage with have something important to share. Each one overcame an obstacle or answered a call from the universe to become a better version of themselves, despite the views of others.

It's been such a privilege to be in contact with all of the writers featured in this book. I hope these stories inspire you, of course, but I also hope they hold you, surround you like a blanket and remind you that you aren't alone. You're sharing the planet with amazing souls who want to same thing as you do. To be acknowledged. To be loved. To be able to say "I Am Here" and have someone else respond, "I See You."

~*Kerri Lowe*
Community Director: StoryShelter

Introduction

The stories in this book were all written and shared on StoryShelter.com. This site was created as a result of an epiphany: Everyone has a story to tell. Writing these stories keeps them alive and sharing these stories makes them valuable.

Each human life represents a fascinatingly rich collection of personal experiences. But with few exceptions, we know little about the compelling life stories of others and they know little of ours. I wanted to change that.

I dreamed of creating a place online that brought these stories together. Thus StoryShelter was born. StoryShelter is a collection of modern day memoirs from everyday people. Our writers answer thought-provoking questions or use our online journal to record memories they don't want to forget and experiences they want to share with others.

As our site grew, I would often read a new story and feel so grateful that I had the opportunity to read about such a compelling experience. There were so many stories that touched my heart, made me laugh and made me think. It seemed natural to collect these favorites and put them in a book for all to enjoy.

This book was a group effort. The authors who have shared here have put their words on paper for all to see and allowed you a glimpse into one of the many experiences that make up who they are. These people all decided to spend their valuable time writing on a new site that wasn't yet well known. We owe our future success to the groundwork our writers have laid down by sharing their stories.

I had little to do with the selecting, compiling and curating of the wonderful stories you are about to read. For that I must thank Kerri Lowe, one of the best storytellers I know. Along with 42 writers, Kerri lets us into her life by sharing a story that has changed who she is and how she views the world. I am honored to work alongside Kerri, and be able to read her stories next to so many others.

We're overjoyed that so many people have used the site as a safe place for self-expression, catharsis, relaxation and entertainment. The compliment we get most often is that the site allows people to get to know themselves, and others, so much better. We hope you enjoy getting to know our friends and we look forward to reading your stories, soon, on StoryShelter.

~Melisa Singh
Founder: StoryShelter

Hidden Passions

"He who has a 'why' to live, can bear
with almost any 'how'."

- Fredrich Nietzsche

A HARLEM NOCTURNE DAYDREAM
Liza Wolfe

"Where words fail, music speaks."
~Hans Christian Andersen

In Psych E-102, Professor Barron droned on and on, "...less obvious characteristics of autism that cause misdiagnoses include awkward social interaction, frequent disambiguation, tactile sensory..."

My gaze floated toward the window, unfocused and unseeing. There were still hours and hours before I could get back home and pick up my saxophone – hours and hours of trying to smile at people...and be polite to people..and having to talk to people...push through the crowds of people, and just...people.

With whom will I play today? Jazz with Charlie Parker? Big Band with Jimmy Dorsey? No, Earl Bostic – definitely Bostic. The song already running through my mind - Harlem Nocturne, an old favorite - an old friend.

I open the burgundy faux-leather case. The faint odors of key oil and cork wax waft out to mix in the air with the lemon verbena candle on the side-table. My hand brushes against the soft brown velvet lining that cushions the bell and cradles the bow. I like the woody taste of the cane reed as I moisten it on my tongue. Removing it, I position the reed on the mouthpiece and tighten the ligature. The pearl insets on the keys are smooth, contrasting with the worn places in the brass finish where my hand has always rested against the cold metal body. My upper teeth slide into the slight groove on the mouthpiece, put there by many, many years of practice. My diaphragm contracts in response to conditioned discipline. A couple of deep controlled breaths – in through the nose and out through the mouth, slow and measured - warm the neck of my horn. I tighten my embouchure and play a purely technical two-and-a-half-octave chromatic scale to warm up.

Leaning to the side, I push the button to start the recording and just let it play, soaking up the soulful melody and fingering the sax's keys in imitation of the famous blues-man. As the song ends, the arm of the old phonograph lifts automatically. Still swaying, still lost in a musician's haze, I return the needle to the vinyl. I close my eyes as it once again begins and let the music move my fingers, easily finding harmonies for the riffs and ad-libs from a long familiarity, melding, melting...

4

Tap, tap, tap on the chalkboard. "Liza! Liza, you're humming... again!" Professor Barron's sharp irritated voice broke through the fog that had settled over my mind. Tap, tap. "The lesson is up here. One more disorder falls into the misdiagnosed autism spectrum. Since we're obviously boring you, I can only assume you already know the answer. Please, Liza, enlighten us."

After several blinks to reacquaint myself with reality, I felt my face flush with embarrassment. Again, all eyes were on me - a few with bored disinterest, a few with eye-rolls and sighs, but most were mocking, accompanied by scoffs and barely muted laughter. I quickly glanced at the incomplete list on the board. Yes, the Prof was right - I knew it well. With downcast eyes, I softly responded, "Asperger's Syndrome. The other one is Asperger's Syndrome."

I heard a slight scratching below me. Looking down at my desk, I saw my fingers still moving in remembered joy.

HOT OFF THE MAT
Shari Eberts

"I never could be good when I was not happy."
~Julia Ward Howe

"Mom, please go to Bikram so we can all have a better day."

This is a direct quote from my 9-year-old son this past Saturday. I was waffling about going to class on Saturday morning since we had a bunch of errands to run and a busy plan for the day. But out of his mouth, came a truism. If I went to a Bikram Yoga class, I would have a better day, and so would the family. The whole family laughed when he said this, and immediately shooed me out the door to class. And we did have a better day - less yelling and frustration, and a lot more laughing and relaxed family time. Ninety minutes very well spent.

That got me thinking about something that teachers often say at the end of class - that the time you take for class is not purely selfish time, but is more than that. Some go as far as to say that taking class is sort of like paying it forward - as the strength and peace you get from class are passed to others you encounter during the day. While I always thought this was somewhat true, my son put it in such simple terms that it really sunk in.

I could always see that going to class was a positive for me - better health, more energy, and a greater sense of calm, but it took my son to show me how it so clearly impacts others in my life as well. We all have a better day when I go to Bikram Yoga class. It's just a fact. I am grateful there is such a simple way to guarantee a better day!

This is the perfect example of how I was never the same after I began practicing Bikram Yoga. I have more energy, a leaner and meaner physique and greater mental clarity. And as you can see from the above story, my children often remind me to go, because I am my better self when practicing Bikram Yoga.

I began practicing almost by accident. I had recently left my job and was looking to get back into shape, but was unwilling to walk too far to get to a workout place. I guess I was feeling lazy. There was a Bikram Yoga studio 3 blocks away, so I thought I would give it a try. I walked in just to take a look and was overwhelmed by the smell of sweat and dripping bodies. As a germaphobe, I thought there was no way this was for me, but somehow I ended up back there the next day for a trial week.

I will never forget my first class. Having never done a yoga class, let alone a Bikram Yoga class, I decided to look the part so I had on yoga pants, a workout tank and a t-shirt. I felt very resourceful as well, having brought my own water bottle with me. I arrived 20 minutes early to fill out paperwork and meet the teacher, Chris. He was exactly what a yoga teacher looked like in my eye - svelte, calm, in control. I felt strong, confident, ready. But then he began to talk. "Your goal for the class is to just stay in the room," he said. "Oh, and you'll need some more water," he mentioned noticing my half drunk small bottle of water. Now I was nervous. If that was really my only goal, then this was going to be harder than I thought...

I set up in the back row in what I was told would be a cool spot. The teacher was a popular one so the class was crowded. I looked around the room and saw men and women of all ages, shapes, sizes and body types. Nice. The room was hot, *very hot*. I was already in a sweat. I took off my t-shirt.

The class began and I followed along as best as I could. My shoulders ached from the breathing exercise, the sweat was running into my eyes, my legs were shaking, but still, I kept at it. Chris explained everything so clearly and the dialogue was so calming, that I just focused on his voice and did my best. By the time we got to the floor series, I was thanking the yoga gods (and Chris!) that I had brought in more than my small bottle of water!

I attempted every posture - attempted being the operative word. By the end of class, I was spent. I had given all that I had and was a puddle of mush on my mat, but I had done it. I felt exhausted, but exhilarated. I felt crazy, but calm. I went home and cried from the sheer exhaustion and effort of it, but then began to feel empowered.

I had done it, and I was going back for more.
The rest, as they say, is history. I have now been practicing for over 5 years and can't imagine my life without it.

What activity couldn't you live without?

WHY I WRITE
Sarah Fader

"O, wonder!
How many goodly creatures are there here!
How beauteous mankind is! O brave new world,
That has such people in't!"
~William Shakespeare (The Tempest)

When I was a teenager, I began struggling with anxiety and depression. I would wake up to my heart racing uncontrollably. My mental health issues were like an annoying person that insisted on tagging along with me everywhere I went. As much as I told the person to go away, she insisted on staying with me. So I learned to live with her, as irritating as she was. She was a nuisance at first, until I began to use her. I learned that the pain that depression caused made me a better artist.

As an adolescent I attended the "Fame" high school in New York City. I was studying theater there. During my sophomore year I played the role of Anne Frank. Also during this time, I was suffering a great deal with clinical depression. I was having trouble eating, showering and functioning. I was in a tremendous amount of emotional pain.

I knew the pain was going to be there no matter what. It was an unwelcome guest, a tagalong and an annoyance. So I used it. As I played the role of Anne Frank, I thought about my emotional agony and I used it to convey how Anne felt. She was trapped. She was in love with Peter, but there was no future for the two of them. Her death was imminent. Her pain was my pain. I became Anne.

I'll never forget that day. I held my scene partner, Nick's, hands, and looked into his eyes searching for something. Earnestly, I thought, *maybe he has the answer to my pain.*

It was the best scene I ever performed during my time at Performing Arts high school. My classmates came up after the scene and congratulated me on my work. Little did they know that the reason that scene was so poignant, the reason that it was emotionally cathartic, was that I was experiencing emotional turmoil. I wasn't myself. I was consumed by a black hole otherwise known as clinical depression.

After graduating high school, I stopped pursuing theater for some time. Unfortunately, that left me with no outlet to express my intense emotions, so I developed an ulcer. I knew that I needed to find an alternative outlet for my emotions that wouldn't wreak havoc on my body. I went in search of what that might be.

Since that time, there have been moments when I've felt hopeless, moments where I've felt my heart pounding so hard I thought my rib cage would explode. There have been times that my entire body was tingling because I'd forgotten to breathe for an indeterminate amount of time. During these moments, I've found a way to release these intense emotions.

Instead of using them to create a theatrical performance, I've transmitted these overpowering emotions into writing. I refuse to let my emotions stay inside of myself. Instead they will pour out of my heart and onto a page where they belong.

Writing provides me with a much-needed release from clinical depression. When I write my feelings on paper, I see what they are. They are no longer overwhelming. They are tangible. I can touch the words. I can read them aloud. I can see that they are just a series of words forming together to become coherent thoughts.

When I feel: I write.
When I write: I release.
When I release: I heal.

YOU ARE TALENTED
Simon Beck

*"Music washes away from the soul
the dust of everyday life."*
~Berthold Auerbach

I remember when we moved the Baldwin into the living room. Bit by bit, piece by piece, it was carted through the front door by strong men in khakis. The three of tiny us sat in our T-shirts and bare feet on the porch swing, Ma brandishing the camcorder while trying to keep us out of their way. They laid the sections on the carpet - still blue and fluffy back then - and built the box that has entertained guests, borne our fury, felt our fingers more than any lover we've had for the past fifteen years.

We didn't have curtains on the windows. We didn't have *curtains*, but we sure as hell had a piano! I approached piano lessons the same way I approached kindergarten: day one was fine, but I cried when I realized this was a regular thing. I hated my lessons. I hated practicing for twenty minutes a day. I hated having theory homework alongside my multiplication tables and spelling words. I hated pulling up to that yellow house on Columbus Avenue and sitting on the scratchy floral couch (orange floral, no less) and learning the damn Suzuki method and being called "SImon" because THAT'S NOT MY NAME.

I told my teacher I was quitting when I was ten. My parents told me I couldn't make that call.
My Ma believed that music lessons would be so beneficial to us in the long-run, which was why she shoved us into those miserable sessions, made us practice the whole time the egg timer was running and ignored our cries of "PLEASE LET US QUIT." Language development, increased IQ, spatial-temporal skills, and improved test scores - says PBS - are all helped by torturing young children with learning "The Happy Farmer" and "Honeybee."

I didn't know it then, but my teacher taught me wrong. For the first few years, when she was introducing a new song to me, she would play sections of it and have me play them back to her. But she didn't realize that I wasn't playing the notes in front of me - I was playing what I heard. It wasn't until my fourth or fifth year of lessons that I actually mastered reading music, seeing notes instead of ants on a grid. And while I always got bad marks in sight-reading at competitions, my ear-reading is top-notch.

I can play anything I hear.

I am not proud of much about myself, but I am proud of that.

Fast-forward to twenty-one-year-old me. My keyboard sits eleven inches from my desk. It's a Roland. A Roland RD-700 SX, to be exact. Apparently the "Cadillac of keyboards." That's what the man at the shop told me when I paraded in there during my junior year of high school, convinced that I was called to be a piano teacher.

For three years after that, when I chose first History then English instead, the keyboard sat in my room at home, collecting dust and bobby pins until I finally wrenched it from the grooves in the carpet and hauled it to my dorm room. And it's killing me now; with two ten-page papers and three essays and two projects and one exam and five performances and two meetings looming over my head, that I can't stop everything and play for an hour.

I miss the twelve years of lessons. I miss coming home from school every afternoon and practicing for twenty, then thirty, then forty, then ninety minutes, until Ma would finally yell, "Remember, you have OTHER things to do!" I miss trekking the mile to the yellow house on Columbus Avenue where I learned how to work hard, to have integrity, to hear what most music students only see. I miss being called "SI-mon" but I don't think it would work if anyone else tried it: it was always the sound of "let's go to work and make a musician out of you."

Music beams my happy. Music holds my sad. Music screams my heart. Music whispers to me, "You are talented."

If you had to go on talent show tomorrow,
what talent would you perform?

Beating the Odds

"Permanence, perseverance and persistence in spite of all obstacles, discouragements and impossibilities: It is this, that in all things distinguishes the strong soul from the weak."

- Thomas Carlyle

HER MOTHER'S DAUGHTER
Keri Yeagley

"When you get into a tight place, and everything goes against you till it seems as if you couldn't hold on a minute longer, never give up then, for that's just the place and time that the tide'll turn."
~*Harriet Beecher Stowe*

I walked into CVS nervously, wandering up and down the aisles, picking up a random item here and there, pretending to examine it before setting it back down again. I wasn't browsing, I knew exactly what I had come into the store for.

Even with the late hour, the store was full of people. Teenage girls laughing and looking at nail polish, tired-looking mothers juggling packs of diapers and squirming infants. I kept my eyes to the floor as I made my way to the last aisle. So many different choices...did it matter which one? I didn't know the difference, but I doubted it could matter. I grabbed a box without really looking and walked quickly back up to the registers. I made my purchase with no eye contact and stuffed it into my purse as I walked out.

At home, I sat back on the closed toilet seat and stared at the stick on the bathroom counter. Two pink lines clear as day, confirming what I already knew. I brought one hand up to my still flat stomach and placed it there, still unbelieving. There was a knock at the door. My mother, not even waiting for an answer, walked right in with a pregnancy test in her hand.

"I want you to take this," she said. My mother, with her own mother's Celtic intuition, bordered on psychic more often than not.

"I don't have to," I answered, with a slight nod towards the counter. The pregnancy test I had already taken sat there telling all. She turned her eyes to the test, nodded at me and walked out.

I was 16, and I had just found out I was pregnant.

It's Friday night, my little one is two, and I'm *exhausted*! You'd think an eighteen year old and a toddler would be equally paired, in energy amounts that is, but alas, they are not! I scoop her out of the tub in her yellow duckie towel and pull the hood up over her wet curls. She smells like heaven and sunshine and a million other sweet things I can't even begin to name.

I powder, diaper and dress her for bed.

An hour later, I sit on the closed toilet seat and lean my head back against the wall. I survey the scene around me. There are little socks and tiny undershirts to add to the laundry pile. There are plastic boats, spongy alphabet letters, and naked Barbies to fish out of the bathtub.

My friends, I'm sure, are just getting ready for a night out...swapping boy stories, sharing shoes, and testing lipstick colors. I stand and take a peek in the mirror as I let the water start to drain. She's still there. The young girl - the funny, outgoing one. The one everyone calls for advice, the beautiful, thoughtful, strong-willed one who never once gave up. She's still there. Her eyes are just a little bit tired now.

I duck my head slightly as I swipe my food stamp card. I would have driven to a store a little further away, less chance of seeing someone we know, but I couldn't spare the gas. Anaya is nine, and with her father gone, things haven't exactly been easy. I thank the cashier and push our cart with the few bags in it out the Wal-Mart doors.

Anaya bounces alongside of me, chattering the way little girls do, about school and friends and TV shows. Clueless to how close to complete devastation we are. She holds her little brother's hand, careful to keep him close. She's always good like that.

The drive home is short. I park the minivan and the kids each take a bag. Inside, I close and lock the front door behind us and switch on the battery-powered lantern I left on the counter.

The electricity was shut off weeks ago. I open up the bag of ice I bought and dump it into the cooler, set up to replace of the stainless steel refrigerator I sold last week to pay for the kids school clothes. After all, what good is a fridge with no electricity?

Anaya helps me unpack the groceries. Milk, cheese, and yogurt go into the cooler. Bread, cereal and peanut butter into the cabinet. It isn't quite that late yet, but it's October and the daylight doesn't last long. The house is big and drafty and once the sun is down it gets chilly fast. I smile at the kids and ask who wants to go upstairs and read stories before bed. I wipe their hands and faces with wet wipes and let them brush their teeth with the gallon jug of water in the bathroom.
We'll bathe at a friend's house in the morning. You forget what a blessing hot water is until you have none!

I layer them up in sweatshirts, sweatpants and socks and we all pile into my big bed together. It keeps them warmer having them sleep here, and honestly, I feel better with them next to me. I read stories by the lantern light until I can tell from the slow, steady breathing that they are asleep. I look down to see

Anaya with her arm draped across her brother, forever the protector.

It's then that I finally let the tears I've been holding in all day begin to fall. I have no idea how I'm ever going to make it through this.

My beautiful, smart, funny and amazingly sarcastic (like her mom!) daughter just turned 15. I look at her sometimes and still can't believe she's mine! I certainly don't feel old enough to have a 15-year-old daughter. I like to tell myself I don't look old enough either! My story turned out better than most. I graduated high school on time with my class and carried my one-year-old baby girl across the stage with me at graduation.

Things weren't always easy. Anaya's dad was sentenced to twenty years in prison when she was nine, leaving me basically alone and broke with Anaya and her siblings. We fell on some very hard times, but I refused to give up. I refused to not give my children a life they could be proud of.

I went back to school, became a nurse, and although we've been through our fair share of trials, we've been okay. I tell my daughter often that most stories don't turn out like mine. I worry as she approaches 16 that she'll fall prey to statistics and become a teenage mother herself. But she has goals and dreams far beyond anything I had imagined for myself at her age and I think she's going to prove the odds wrong once again.

She is after all, her mother's daughter.

THE THIRD CHOICE
Carol Graham

"Keep you face always toward the sunshine – and shadows will fall behind you."
~Walt Whitman

I was born with health issues that were often debilitating and caused me to wonder if my life would be cut short by disease. I watched my mother suffer my entire life, and before my eighteenth birthday I said goodbye to her for the last time.

My monthly periods were dreadful. The pain was so intense that my entire body would become contorted. It was like my entire nervous system seized and I lost all control because of unbearable pain. I saw several specialists but there were no answers. Then I got the phone call from a gynecologist's office informing me he had a diagnosis. That conversation changed my life. There is one word in any language that is difficult to hear. That word is -- cancer.

It rolled off his tongue far too easily. I could not form my lips to even utter it. I was a young woman in my twenties. I was trembling and frightened.

"Carol, basically you have two choices and I think it is obvious which one you will choose!"

I assumed he meant two types of treatment. He continued, "Your choices are hysterectomy or death." He paused for impact. "You are a very sick young woman." He seemed far too nonchalant about the whole matter.

Strength I did not know I had welled up inside of me and I said "I do not accept those choices. There has to be another way! I will find that alternative."

Rage overcame him. I had challenged his intelligence. He rose up from behind his desk, leaned towards me and pointed his finger in my face. He was so angry he was shooting spit when he said, "Well then, lady, go home, suffer and.......die!"

I stood up, spun on my heel and started out of the room. Then I paused, turned, and said in a loud staccato voice, enunciating each syllable clearly.

"I...will...walk...in...here...pregnant...one...day."
I couldn't believe the words that came out of nowhere. But in my heart, I knew I was going to succeed.

Nothing was going to stop me. I almost screamed out loud "ENOUGH, not this time." *Hysterectomy? I don't think so. Death? Not my time yet.*

A seed of personal power was planted in my heart as a little girl, and the more I nurtured it, the stronger it became. My father told me I could feed my fears or feed my faith. The choice was mine.

About three weeks after I had seen the doctor, I attended a food supplement demonstration in a friend's home. I was amazed at all the information the woman had to offer regarding our food and how it was processed. The more I listened, the more hope I felt. Could this be my answer?

I purchased my bag of hope and started my new regime of food supplements. In less than a week I was feeling better. Even if I never felt any more improvement, it was worth my investment to feel this good for a few days. That simple little house meeting I attended started me on a whole new road of health awareness. It became my passion for the last forty years.

I researched each product, took every course on nutrition I could find and was determined to improve my health. There was no doubt whatsoever that God had directed my path.

It was the middle of March, fourteen years later, when I made an appointment with the same doctor. My health had improved so much and I was doing my best to remain composed. Inside, my stomach was doing flip-flops.

"Hello, Carol. It has been a while since I have seen you. Why did you decide to come now?" I couldn't believe how old he looked. He seemed to have aged much more than 14 years.

"I haven't had a physical for a long time and figured I should." I began to imagine what he would say if I were actually pregnant. And what would *I* say?

He examined me, left the room and said he would return shortly when he got the lab results from my urine sample. It was 1:12 P.M. I wondered how long a few minutes would be as I stared at the clock and watched it move ever so slowly. One minute, then two. Five minutes went by. Ten minutes, then fifteen. It was a full half hour when the doctor walked back into the examining room.

"Carol, I am very sorry to inform you, but you are very pregnant." His head was down as if he were ashamed.

I stood up. "Yes, doctor, I...am...sure...you...are... very…sorry…to....inform...me.   You   obviously remember the words you spoke to me the last time I was here. What do you have to say about that?"

I was not prepared in any way for the next words that came out of his mouth. Trying to gain his

28

composure and his rightful position, he stood up and whispered a shout, "Who is the father?" He threw the words at me, the same way he had all those years ago.

I thought maybe, just maybe, he would apologize to me or even be happy for me. I never expected him to be angry.

He must have remembered, or read it in my file, that Paul was sterile. However, Paul had received a report some months earlier of healthy sperm. There was no way I was going to waste my breath by telling the doctor. I wanted out of his awful room that reeked of pharmaceuticals. I made a waving gesture with my hands indicating I wanted to get dressed. He left and I never saw him again.

When Paul saw me, I thought he was going to cry. I didn't have to say a word.

Without any warning, my reserved, conservative husband stood up on a chair, cupped his hands around his mouth, and made a trumpet-like announcement to the hundred plus people in the room. "MY...WIFE...IS...GOING.........TO........HAVE.........A BABY!"

He was grinning like a little kid who had just performed an act that made him very proud of himself. I wanted to laugh and cry. The news genuinely hit – I was going to have a baby.

Our baby girl was born in 1986 and three years ago, I became a grandma. Over the years, I have helped countless women realize optimum health and give birth to babies they were told they would never have. It all began with a determination to succeed…and the will to never let go of it.

What is the most difficult challenge you've faced in your lifetime?

JOURNEYMAN
John Vercher

*"He has not learned the first lesson of life who does not every
day surmount a fear."*
~John Dryden

Trying to find your identity growing up is rarely easy,
but discovering who you are as a biracial child is more
difficult still. I didn't talk like the most of the black kids
and I didn't look like most of the white kids. I became
so gifted at the mimicry of dialects that it became a
subconscious act. I would do anything to fit in. Change
my clothes, change my attitude. The trend continued
on into my early adulthood. All the while, my weight
spiraled out of control and I developed a crippling
anxiety that threatened to consume me.

In 2005, I caught hold of a lifeline. A reality show
about mixed martial arts launched its inaugural season

on a fledgling cable channel. Every Thursday night, I was transported back to the living room carpet of my childhood home, where I laid on my stomach with my chin in my hands, basking in the glow of Saturday morning Kung Fu Theater. When I watched the reality show fights, I felt something stir. I saw men with stories like mine who used their anger, and their psychological and physical scars, to become warriors. One night I watched in bed as my wife's gentle snores warmed my arm wrapped around her. The credits rolled after a particularly thrilling episode and I nudged her.

"Babe," I said. "I want to fight."

She stirred but never opened her eyes. "That's good, sweetie."

And for the next nine years, fight I did. Through injury. Through frustration. Through fear and self-doubt. And finally in the ring and in the cage. My fists, shins and heart became the instruments with which I wrote my new story. It began like this:

"Maybe if I shit my pants, they'll cancel the fight." I deliberated on that notion for well over a minute, which is at least fifty-five seconds longer than any rational adult should ponder intentionally defecating in another man's automobile. But it felt like my best and only option. What talked me out of it was not the idea that to do so was base and disgusting. It was because I knew that all it would result in was an embarrassing clean up and I would still have to fight, smelling like excrement.

Coach reached the exit to Fleetwood, Pennsylvania, where certain pain and humiliation awaited me. He slowed his jet black WRX enough that throwing myself out the door would only lead to mild road rash. I was screwed.

We parked at the field house, retrieved my gear bag from the trunk and walked towards the entrance. The October air was crisp and chilled my lungs with each nervous breath. We pushed through the heavy double doors. The field house gym engulfed us in a cloud of humidity and stale sweat. We made our way to the backstage area to wrap my hands and begin my warm ups. That was when I saw him.

He looked normal enough. His coach held the focus mitts and his punches detonated with each strike. My heart dislodged from my chest and landed with a splash in my innards. His trainer offered him water during a break in his drills, but he pushed it aside. Instead, he reached into a box and devoured a small live puppy. He then sprouted horns and smiled at me with sanguineous fangs. (It's far more likely that he ate a protein bar, donned his headgear and put in his mouthpiece...but I saw what I saw.)

I choked back a mouthful of bile as I walked towards the ring. Coach held open the ropes for me as I

33

ascended the wooden steps to the ring of death. There was no turning back. He fastened the chin strap on my headgear, turned me by my shoulders and pushed me to the center of the ring for the stare down. I tried to look everywhere but my opponent's eyes, but for a millisecond, our gazes met. In that brief instant, I saw in him a glimmer of the same fear that was making my hands go numb. Or maybe it was just my reflection.

The bell rang and we ran to the center. He threw a right hook that came from his knees and a kaleidoscope of colors exploded behind my eyes and in that moment, I understood with celestial clarity our hard-wired response of fight-or-flight.

Suddenly, my Tyler Durden appeared as a single frame in the film reel of my life and shrugged as if to ask me, "Which will it be?" I fought. For three rounds we put on the ugliest display of kickboxing known to man. Limbs flew akimbo, punches were thrown with reckless abandon and we ripped open our chests to reveal our beating hearts for the crowded field house to see. And it was glorious.

MY BEAUTIFUL OBSESSION
Kaitlyn Maiani

"I try to avoid looking forward or backward, and try to keep looking upward."
~Charlotte Bronte

My freshman year in college, I developed an eating disorder that almost took away my life.

I was training for a marathon when it started. I had gotten a partial softball scholarship for college, but struggled with self-doubt and frustration as I saw girls less talented than me play all the games while I was benched. I decided to quit softball and transfer schools. That's when I took up running. I had never felt so focused or wanted something so badly in my life until I started racing.

While training for my first marathon, I became obsessed with running, my weight, and controlling my food. I did not have any intentions of letting myself get so thin, but it just happened. I got through the marathon despite the physical problems I was developing from not getting enough food, but it was tough. I started having pains in my chest and even fainting frequently while training for my second, but that still wasn't enough to stop me from restricting my food. Finally, after the biggest scare of my life, I knew I needed help.

I was running on one of my training runs in the summer when it was about 90 degrees outside. Around the sixteenth mile I became light-headed, short of breath, and physically could not talk. I knew that something wasn't right and that I'd have to stop. By the time that I made it to the Krispy Kreme Donuts bathroom nearby, I was foaming from the mouth. I looked into the mirror and was horrified by the reflection that was staring back at me. I do not remember much after that because I collapsed right there in the bathroom. All I can remember was waking back up and being completely out of it. I splashed some water on my face and ran off to finish the last 5 miles. When I got home I knew that I needed to tell my family what had happened, but I couldn't bring myself to do so. It was not until after I started treatment that I was able to finally tell my mom what had happened that day.

After that incident I knew there was something physically wrong with my body, but I didn't want to face it. My mom had her own worries however, and insisted that I go to an eating disorder treatment center. I didn't want to "recover," but I went to the appointment simply to appease her. When I came into the office, I felt a flood of emotions. The 'healthy' Kaitlyn knew I needed to be there, but the 'disordered' Kaitlyn was raging.

First, I was sent to the examination room to take all of my vitals. The nurse didn't seem surprised by them, so it made me feel like 'Yes, I'm going to breeze through this appointment.' Little did I know that my low weight and dangerous vital signs could have put me into the hospital. I can remember my doctor's exact words, "Kaitlyn your heart is just going to give out on you when you are sleeping, and you are just not going to wake up." Those words to a normal person would scare the living daylights out of them, but to me, it still wasn't enough to make me stop. I said what I needed to to appease the doctor, and he let me go.

I continued running and training for another three months with monthly check ups in-between. Stepping on the scale showed that I was continuing to lose more weight, and my vitals continued to fall lower and lower. On my last scheduled appointment with my doctor, he advised my mother that she needed to make me go for a more thorough eating disorder evaluation.

July 15th was my evaluation day at the eating disorder clinic. The doctor took my vitals and was so scared to let me leave that he said I had two choices, and I wasn't going to like either one of them. He told me that I had to enter the inpatient treatment the following day, or get admitted at that very moment. He knew that if I didn't get treatment immediately that I wouldn't have made it back to my next monthly appointment because my parents would have been burying me. Looking back, that was the moment my life was saved, but it was also the moment where my world turned upside down.

All of my freedom was taken away the second I entered treatment. I no longer had any choice about what I ate, when I ate, how much I could eat, if I could workout, or anything else. I felt like I was a five-year old again trapped in a twenty-two-year-old's body. I went from negative net calories a day, to surpassing what I used to consume in an entire week. The feeling of fullness was overwhelming, but I continued to push through. Each day seemed to get harder because I had to eat more, and do less. Before this, I was not a person to sit and relax. I did not know what those two words meant, nor would I allow myself to learn the definition of them.

After entering treatment, I was fully exposed to

what relaxation meant. It felt like we sat the entire day and exercise was forbidden. It was nice to go to arts n' crafts, or attend group therapy, but I still felt as if I was the laziest person in the whole entire world. As the weight started to come on strong, I felt less and less interested in hanging out with friends. My relationship with my boyfriend seemed to come to a pretty bad standstill, as I hated the fact that I was not 'as pretty, or as skinny' as I was before. Sadly, putting on weight was actually what my boyfriend had wanted the whole time. Anorexia is a disease that messes with your mind, making you believe everything that it wants you to believe.

I was in treatment for three long months. Each day was a different obstacle, whether it was reintroducing a certain food group, or learning how to accept not fitting into old clothes anymore. Many times I would sit in front of my mirror and just bawl my eyes out because I hated the reflection that it produced. It was not until my mom had me write on my mirror "You are beautiful" that I finally looked into the mirror with some kind of confidence. But some things would shake that confidence. The more that people would say "you look healthy," or "you look so much better," the worse I felt because I knew what those comments really indicated. They meant that people could now see that I was gaining weight, and to me that meant I was getting fat. I still struggle today with this concept and such compliments are hard to accept. That said, I feel so much more confident than I used to - not just with my looks but with everything in my life. The perfectionism has decreased, my ability to focus and concentrate has increased, and I'm a much happier person.

The treatment program saved my literal life, but it also brought back the life that the true Kaitlyn (the girl I was *before* my eating disorder) lost during the four years that she suffered with anorexia. My journey to recovery never would have started if not for my absolutely amazing mother. She saw me better than I could see myself, and for that I am truly blessed.

FAR FROM THE CROWD
Bertram Allan Mullin

"Saying nothing...sometimes says the most."
~Emily Dickinson

I was supposed to die three years ago during several necessary back operations. Without them I'd be crippled, or worse. Throughout middle school and into adulthood I was shrinking, bending, and hunched over. My spine wouldn't stop winding downward like some Slinky, crushing me.

My muscles were screwed. I couldn't smile without feeling prickling shots of pain from my spine. My shoulder blades felt like they had hooks pulling me down with every step. Everyone thought I was depressed. The only emotions I knew how to express without hurting were "pain," "anger," and "frustration." There I was, "hopeless."

No scoliosis surgeon in Houston would touch me. One day, I saw an ad for a spine doctor in Dallas. He held the title: The Man Who Wrote the Book on the Back. I shortened it to "Spine God." He could fix me.

I was so bad off I could hardly walk by 2011. I used a cane to help me stand while my back crushed me from within. Instead of looking like Quasimodo, I appeared way shorter than I should have been. My real height was 5'8, and I was slouched down to 5'3. A free bonus included scars from stretch marks from when my bones would slide awkwardly against my skin. Falling was a regular part of life. All I had to look forward to was seeing Manda, my best friend, my more. The one who would help me stand, and the first to care. Whenever she was around I could ignore the pain. Gain a bit of focus.

But I had to let her go before I died during the operations. What kind of man kept a woman around when he knew he might die?

I never saw Manda cry over me, and I didn't intend to. First, I had to have a consult with the Spine God and find out if the odds of dying were really as glum as I calculated. If not, I could keep seeing her.

Most conversations were blurry then. There was no way to recall verbatim what the Spine God said. Like looking through steam, it was near impossible to see past the fog of pain. He told me, *Doctor jargon.*

Semantics. More doctor stuff. Rods. Screws. Rebuild you. I started to hear the Six Million Dollar Man theme for a minute. Then I refocused.

Rhubarb. Did he really say that? It felt like I was stabbed with an electric bolt up my spine a second ago.

Eight operations to fix you. Elsewise you'll be crippled or dead. Those were definitely his words. *You'll need a few years to recover, and will have trouble bending. Pilates and physical therapy might help.*

The difference between me and other surgeons, I used to build houses. A good builder starts with every brick, every layer, never cutting corners. I'll build your house so that it's livable again.

It sounded great.

You might die. Risk. Danger. Scary words. My hot nurses will get with you on writing a will and all that jazz. If he really referred to his nurses as "hot" and said, "all that jazz," it made him pretty cool, but it was probably an illusion brought on from the pain again...

I dealt with my will, said hidden hard goodbyes to friends, and readied myself to say farewell to the most important one.

Manda and I had been hanging out for two years. It was difficult to feel how I felt for her when other girls would look at me like I was deformed. Manda made me feel wanted.

We had tea and dinner together at this quiet place called "Far From the Crowd," based off the Hardy book. Thomas Hardy was the owner Quey's favorite author, but she added her uniqueness to the name.

Manda loved how quiet the place was. Silent moments to her were like kisses.

"Why don't you pick the flavor this time?" She shoved her shoulder against mine. I was so frail, even that hurt. I couldn't let her know.

"Jasmine. Makes you smile," I said.

"Putting me on the spot like that doesn't," she said. Manda moved her librarian glasses back. Her bright blue eyes became twice the size. "Just pick a flavor," she told me.

"Something dark."

"What?"

Quey kept grinning at us. "Are you ready to order?"

"Yeah. Dark tea."

"Which-a-one?" Quey asked. "We have Earl Grey, Irish, Masala Chai, and English afternoon." She held a pot with one hand and wiped her counter down with the other.

"Masala." Sounds exotic.

"Finally," Manda sighed. We sat. "Not so hard to make a choice. Is it?"

44

"About that . . . " I looked down. "Do you want food, too?"

"I'm not hungry. Think I'll just write poetry in my notebook. Unless there's something you want to talk about."

She had the greatest sense of woman's intuition. Why was this so hard? I hadn't said I loved her. I hadn't yet let myself. If I did and then died, she'd carry that with her the rest of her life.

Maybe I could get all creepy with her? Say something insane. That would scare her off. Lying wasn't my style though.

The tea came. I could smell the steam as it rubbed my face and watched it become our smoky divider. Manda allowed the aroma to settle under her nostrils. "I like this."

My taste buds weren't really all there. I relished anything she enjoyed because being near her, having someone who mattered to me, was all I needed, and here she was, "Manda?"

"Yes?"

"Remember when we met? How we'd joke about hanging out until we read the books and saw all three of those Stieg Larsson films? We're done with the novels. And we watched *The Girl with the Dragon Tattoo*, *The Girl Who Played with Fire*, and last week *The Girl Who Kicked the Hornet's Nest*."

"Get to the point before I make a new one: *The Girl Who Kicked the Boy in the Nuts*."

She was half kidding, half threatening, but I chuckled. It was hard not to laugh when she smiled at me. "Just—"

Manda's eyebrow raised a light bulb kind of rise. "You know what I love about Larsson's writing the most? It's not what's said, but what's *unsaid* that's so important."

"Manda."

"Don't say any more. Just tell me. When are your operations?"

So she figured me out. "February."

"Will you have someone with you?"

"My brother and cousins from Houston to Austin are coming to Dallas in shifts."

"Good." Manda stared into my eyes as though to remember what they looked like.

I memorized Manda from her long golden locks to her everlasting grin, so I'd know all of her details down to each birthmark.

I had the operations, and through rigorous physical therapy recovered fully within a year.

There I was . . . alive. There I was . . . able to smile and look at myself in the mirror and say with focus, "I am here."

It felt a little empty without her . . .

At least we had our unsaid moments, far from the crowd.

What's the biggest risk you've ever
taken in your lifetime?

In retrospect, would you take it again?

Adventures

"When we try to pick out anything by itself, we find it hitched to everything else in the universe."

- John Muir

THE RIDE OF A LIFETIME
Jennifer Wolfe

"A man who dares to waste one hour of time has not discovered the value of life."
~ *Charles Darwin*

We loaded into the back of the small, dilapidated, white Toyota pickup truck. No safety restraints were in sight, unless the roll bars along the top counted. Eight children aged 6 to 14 years couldn't believe their good fortune. Eight adults searched each other's faces for solidarity. This went against all our instincts, but so did waking up in a Nicaraguan compound with an armed guard standing at the door.

It seemed like a good idea at the time. Although native English speakers, my kids had only ever attended school in Spanish. They had no choice about it – from kindergarten on, they attended a public Spanish

Immersion elementary school and quickly became fluent.

At first, the road started out dusty but flat. As we pulled out from behind the large black iron gates, I knew I was embarking on something that would take me far, far out of my comfort zone. Dressed in shorts, t-shirt, sturdy shoes, bandanas, and hats to protect us from the blazing sun, I wondered how hard could it be? I had plenty of fresh water and granola bars in my backpack. Two bottles of hand sanitizer – one in my pocket and a backup in my pack – would prevent any illness. Our daily doses of malaria medication and enough industrial strength DEET bug spray to kill all the bugs in Nicaragua would keep us from insect driven disease.

As the pickup truck left town, I relaxed a bit. Beaming smiles of bliss radiated from each child – there was no fear on their faces. Moving slowly down the dirt road we waved as we passed children and parents beginning their days in their humble, dirt-floored homes. Cement walls created a shelter for them, and chickens and skinny dogs sauntered in and out. Wisps of smoke rose from the outdoor fire pits. Broad, white grins mixed with confused countenances met our white-skinned faces and shouts of greeting – not many 'chelles' in this part of the world.

The tiny truck wound its way down the road, the

homes spreading further and further apart. A caballero and his companion greet our driver as he slows to a halt, carefully avoiding the emaciated cows on the road. Relationships are key to survival in this part of the world. The adults grab their cameras and snap away, most never having seen a real cowboy at work before. The kids smile broadly in disbelief.

Sparse, green grassland dotted with the occasional tree line both sides of the road. Every few miles family home vegetable gardens interrupted the rocky outcroppings. Undeterred, the farmers work around them.

Slowing to a halt, we notice a wrinkled old man on the side of the road. Victor, our driver, calls out a greeting and waves him closer. The man approaches the back of the truck, and I realize he intends to squeeze in with us. As he throws one arm over the side and carefully enters the pickup bed, his two-foot long machete enters with him. Our young American sons' eyes widen in disbelief at the weapon within arm's reach. The old American parents' eyes widen in momentary panic.

Continuing up the road, local Nicaraguans looking for a ride repeatedly greet us. No one turned away; we realize the amazing opportunity to meet them up close and personal as we squish back to back and side to side in the shrinking truck.

The truck takes a sharp left turn and wheels begin to spin. Victor, unphased, eases it into low gear and we begin to climb a hill. The flat road has disappeared, replaced by small rocks at first, then enormous boulders. The adults begin to bark safety directions and plan for the eventual rollover. The truck lurches to the right, and I yelp in terror. The boys fist pump in jubilation, and we find ourselves right side up.

After an eternity, we make one last turn and the tiny pickup groans and lurches to a halt. As I wait for my brain to stop spinning and my heartbeat to ease, a sound like thunder reaches my ears. Children, teens and adults begin to crowd around, pulling on the doors and grinning widely. The entire community is cheering and screaming as if Justin Bieber has just walked on stage, when in reality it is just me - shy, unsure, vulnerable- and 15 other Americans about to continue the ride of a lifetime in Nicaragua.

FREE RUNNING
Jim Ross

"Why the hell not?"
~Anonymous

When I was a year out of college, I went to the beach in Wilmington, NC, for a week with my parents and the younger of my two brothers. We rented a big house right on the perfectly smooth, flat NC beach. It looked like nearly every other house on the beach: a box covered with well-weathered shakes. My norm in those days was to run in the morning and again in the evening.

However, one night, I woke up at about 3 a.m. and decided to go run on the beach in the dark. The beach had a nice clean surface, so running barefoot wasn't an issue.

Since it was pitch dark, and there were no signs of life, I decided to run on the beach naked. I wasn't in the habit of doing this. I'd never done it before. It was just a perfect night. I was driven by the thought that few things in life could bestow a sense of freedom comparable to running on a perfect beach in your birthday clothes.

I ran for about 20 minutes when I decided it was time to turn around and head back to the house. After about 10 or 15 minutes, I decided to start looking for the house. Not until then did it strike me: all the houses looked identical, especially in the dark.

The odds were close to zip that I could pick out the right house on the first try. And I couldn't very well start picking out houses at random, because if I picked the wrong house, which I almost certainly would, a variety of suboptimal scenarios were likely to develop. Most of them involved getting arrested. At that point, in my wildest dreams, I couldn't imagine a positive scenario for walking into the wrong house naked. Though in hindsight, there was a slim chance of getting laid, or at least being offered a beer and a pillow.

I decided to be discreet by remaining in the water until the rosy-fingered dawn first poked over the horizon. I made my way slowly along the beach in chest-high water, hoping to find some way of distinguishing the house and making a run for it.

Before dawn, the fishermen and women started to show up, staked their territory, and cast their lines out into the ocean. Fortunately, none of them saw me, or they did and decided to steer clear. As the first signs of dawn could be seen on the horizon, I was still trying to find some way of distinguishing our house from all the houses that looked just like it.

Finally, when light was cast over everything, but before the sun broke the horizon, I was able to make out my father's car. I waded toward the beach using my hands like a propeller and tore across the beach to our house. I didn't give a damn whether any of the people out fishing saw me. Fortunately, nobody else at the house was up yet, especially my mother, so I didn't have any explaining to do. When I think back to that night, I think of it now as the perfect run.

ON THE TOWER
Judie Hathaway

"Why I'd like nothing better than to achieve some bold adventure, worthy of our trip."
~Aristophanes

Most people remember the more traumatic moments in their lives, and strangely enough, those events become their most cherished memories. My most traumatic event occurred on a trip up the Eiffel Tower in Paris.

My traveling companion and best friend, Joe, alternately encouraged and shamed me as I resisted his offer to take me to the top of this enduring pride of Paris. Having suffered a fear of crowds and heights my entire life, I was not about to go to the top, or for that matter, any of the tower's three levels. This work of art did not look secure enough for one person, let alone an entire fleet of bug-eyed tourists!

But the day we were to leave Paris, I reluctantly surrendered to Joe's constant urging. After having a glass of strong red wine at a picturesque outdoor café, we approached the tower. With a foreboding of doom, I tried to think of any way to run away, ideally with dignity. Too late. Without looking up, we boarded the hulking, open-caged elevator and I had nothing less than a death grip on Joe's hand. With his reassuring comfort, I gradually began to adjust to the cramped surroundings, but as the massive door began to rattle shut, an entire busload of tourists pushed into what little breathing space still existed. I attempted to escape, but the excited and determined groups of people were pushing inward and I was trapped.

Compressed to the center of the elevator, I lost my grip on Joe. There was no room to move or even breathe. Just before a scream could escape my mouth, we reached the top of the tower with a sharp jolt and stopped. The door slowly rattled open, and the mass of people pushed me out of the cage. I grabbed the nearest pillar holding on with every fiber in my being. I quickly became aware that I was standing on a sweeping, steel-grated platform and below me was the entire city of Paris. It was as though I was on the outside of an airplane.

Joe eventually found me attempting to sit close to a wall, still clinging to what I had begun to think of as "my pillar." Joe has a look that can turn his soft blue eyes into a deep, piercing cold blue. No one would even think to defy him at these times. "Get up" he said. Reluctantly, and very slowly, I took his hand as he helped me up.

Cautiously, we inched our way along the inside wall of this astounding tower. We read all the stories of how and why this amazing structure exists. Soon, my intense fear began to evaporate enough to enjoy the history of the brave people who constructed it. Obviously, this was a most remarkable construction feat, especially in the time of its production.

With some guidance from Joe, I was able to carefully creep to the edge. It was then I experienced a truly profound moment. While my eyes scanned that panoramic view, a warm feeling began as a small dot of intense light in my spirit. There was a strange "knowing" that this event would somehow always be a part of me.

The endless view of Paris sparkled brilliantly below. The scene before me was reminiscent of rare jewels in many shades of silver, sparks of blue, slashes of yellow and traces of red. The black sky displayed what seemed to be at least 10 trillion stars. The setting sun highlighted several thin, three-dimensional silver jet trails in the distance, which added to my complete astonishment at this memorable moment. Softly, and very quietly, my emotions spilled over and deep tears seemed to clean a place in my spirit that had been covered in grime. Washed clean, I was certain that I would never view life with hopelessness again. There are so many beautiful things in this world!

As I reflect to that magical time in Paris, it is clear that the tower does look very much like a fragile lacework of steel beams and cables. And yet, despite its delicate appearance, the tower has supported hundreds of thousands of bodies throughout the years. Joe forced me to walk through my fear and now, when I think of that magical moment, I know that nothing is as bad as I think it is.

I am far more able to put my fear aside and enjoy life. This is a new kind thinking for me, one that never occurred before I first visited the City of Light, and courageously faced that bone-chilling fear.

PASSPORTS

Connie Gross

*"For my part, I travel not to go anywhere, but to go.
I travel for travel's sake. The great affair is to move."*
~Robert Louis Stevenson

Passports - the secret to foreign lands, grand adventures, and exciting opportunities. I saw hundreds of foreign passports while working as a summer immigration officer. I loved stamping them, knowing that I was leaving a permanent record for someone - a sign that they had indeed been approved for entry into Canada. Perhaps my excitement about the stamp was more about my signature, and recognizing that someday someone would look at that signature and know that I played a part in their journey.

That summer I saw passports from many countries. Most of them shared the same blue cover and symbols indicating a member of the Commonwealth. But others came in different colours and insignias, showing that they came from a place very different from mine. I even saw the elusive red documents belonging to diplomats.

Of course in my young mind they were off to do very important missions, so secret that I couldn't begin to imagine the intrigue behind their visit. Most of them were probably on minor administrative duties, or taking a quick break from their American assignments. Nevertheless, they still captured my imagination.

For the two summers I worked at the border, I longed to have my own passport so that I too could start collecting stamps from around the world. When I finally booked my overseas trip and received my first passport, I was ecstatic. I felt like I was finally a grown up about to start the real adventures in life.

I still have that passport tucked away in my trunk. Although I only took a few trips that needed that passport, I still treasure that book of memories. Today I have a new passport, and have started a new phase in my life. I finally made it to Europe a few years ago when I chaperoned my son's high school trip. Even though the European Union's border agreement meant quick access across borders, I was still irked that I came home with only a couple of passport stamps.

Similarly, although I am glad that the law requiring Canadians to show passports when entering the U. S. A. hasn't really slowed down the border crossing process, I still am a little disappointed when the American Customs Officer hands my passport back to me without stamping it.

My desire for travel has not dimmed. I still want to collect those wonderfully exciting visa stamps - signs of grand adventures and entrance to foreign lands. I still pay attention to the signatures on my passport and hope that somewhere out there, someone is looking at their old passport and noticing mine!

DAD WOULD APPROVE
Mattea Kramer

"Not until we are lost do we begin to understand ourselves."
~Henry David Thoreau

We walked out the door and blinked into the sun. There was a line of shiny black Mercedes along with the bright yellow taxicabs on the street. But we waited for bus number 34, like the guidebook said.

These were our first moments in Nairobi, Kenya.

A thing I did a lot of, after Dad died, was backpack around the world. After college I lived behind a Jack-in-the-Box and worked in restaurants and political campaigns to save up some money. And then I went to Nepal. And then to India. And then to Kenya. For part of it, I was traveling with my brother.

Because he, also, spent a lot of time wandering after Dad died. Probably everyone wanders after loss, it's just that some people wander metaphorically and some people pack a bag and wander physically.

A thing that was great about traveling with my brother was that sometimes I'd get run down from being on the road and staying in dirt-cheap places and spending eighteen hours on a train or a bus or whatever. And so every once in a while, I'd want to stay at a decent hotel and have a good hot shower and a bed with nice fresh sheets. And what my brother would say to that was, "Dad would approve."

Dad wasn't one to rough it, was what my brother meant by that. Dad was more of a nice-hotel-with-a-fitness-center type guy. And so every once in a while, my brother and I would get ourselves a decent hotel and have that good warm feeling of a hot shower and a clean place to stay. And we'd talk about how Dad would approve. And that feeling of Dad's approval was the most comforting thing of all.

And I was steeled and fortified by it. So that afterward, we ventured out into the unknown.

By which I mean, we went on a budget safari. I say "budget" because an actual safari costs a pretty penny. So we took public transit to the entrance of the only Kenyan national park that you can enter on foot; you can go in without a safari Land Rover or any vehicle at all.

Now, it's true that there was a very slim chance we'd happen upon a lion. Very slim chance. Even on a high-end safari way out in the bush, it's a rare precious thing to stumble upon a lion. But if we *did* meet a lion, that's the situation in which we'd have really missed that pricey Land Rover, plus the accompanying guards with tranquilizer darts, or guns, or whatever it is they carry.

So I guess if we'd come across a lion we'd have said something like, "Mrs. Lion, I was told it was very unlikely that I'd meet you."

Don't worry, though. We didn't see any lions.

But we did walk among the wild giraffes.

What has been your favorite place
to travel so far?

Overcoming Obstacles

"The greater the obstacle,
the more glory in overcoming it."

- Moliere

BAREFOOTIN'

Tex Parker

"I am not young enough to know everything."
~Oscar Wilde

Summertime, and the livin' is - - - in the air-conditioned house; boys watching electronic screens.

Poor Dears, can't let them get a heat stroke or sweaty.

Not many boys going barefoot anymore. Unsanitary and unsightly. No shoes, No service. Tender feet can't step on a grass burr; hurts.

Girls seldom were barefoot at school. So un-lady-like. By the time boys started to notice girls, they were all too grown-up and cool to let their feet stick out in the aisles of classrooms.

1954; Elvis records his first hit; "That's Alright Little Mama," Bill Haley and the Comets do "Rock

Around the Clock," Big Joe Turner cuts "Shake Rattle and Roll." Birth of Rock and Roll, Baby.

America's premier female athlete was Babe Didrikson Zaharias. Golf, basketball, track, pool, she did it all; even recorded some hit songs on the Mercury label.

A nuclear test on Bikini Island leaves a giant hole in the water where land once was. At Wright's Drug Store on North Shepherd in Houston Heights the latest soda-jerk/delivery boy was a handsome eighth grader named Dal Parker (one of the many handles your much older but still semi-attractive writer has used).

Wright's was around the corner from Love Elementary where I had attended and was still teaching Gerry, my little brother.

Doc Wright would hire a Junior High boy to work the fountain and make deliveries. It was a prestigious and important job. They had to be at least in the seventh grade and usually would not stay past the ninth; when riding a bike making deliveries became un-cool.

Hamilton Junior High was two miles from Love and I had to ride like the Devil with a tail wind to beat the younger kids to the counter. Mostly I arrived a few minutes after they were seated, rudely clicking coins on the marble counter top.

The race to the best seat was usually won by a boy

in Mrs. Nichols' fifth grade class; it was by the door and even though the sixth grade boys were older and faster, their room was down the hall and a head start made the difference.

The coveted stool was where I would start serving the customers. Nickel Cokes and ice cream cones were the usual orders. I'd go down the counter and ignore the coin clickers. All in good time. Wait your turn, no pushing. Most would get their order and go; make room for a new buyer.

March 1, 1954 was a Monday and the first official day of barefootin' at Love; per Mrs. Simmons, Principal.

Kids got a new pair of leather soled shoes for back-to-school and the rough playing boys would wear theirs out by Spring. Parents felt it a waste to buy new ones; just wait until Fall.

I arrived that day surprised to see eleven year old Mary June Gerig sitting patiently in the first position with a huge smile.

Next to her was big Toby Hanz, who had failed his grade level several times and was usually the daily winner. Toby waited a while getting to the fifth grade where he shaved daily and drove his own car to school. Next down the line were his cousins; the evil Cooper twins.

Bad boys all; they glared at the winner, muttering evil thoughts and threats. How mortifying to be beaten by some girl. Had never happened before.

I'll have a Chocolate Soda, please, she said, smiling past too big for her face, fully grown adult front teeth. All the customers groaned, it took time to create a soda. Aw, come on, they whined, I gotta get home. Hurry up.

Grab a soda glass, put in a little vanilla ice cream and a shot of chocolate syrup, squish it around with a long spoon. A hit from the fizz side of the soda faucet, then two scoops of vanilla, fill the glass with soda from the slow side. Whipped cream and cherry? I asked.

Oh, yes, please do, she replied.

Two cherries for you, I said, returning her smile, thirty-five cents, please.

She slowly unwrapped a fifty-cent piece from a lace-edged hanky and goes, with an even bigger smile, You may keep the change.

Oh, thank you, I bowed and replied, The Lord loves a good tipper. The other kids all looked away at that.

Doc Wright had told me all the young girls were in love with the soda fountain boy and I should act accordingly. Good for business, he allowed.

The Good Doc taught me a lot about business, and people too. When you go on a delivery, he said, it's usually not important. Life Magazine or today's Chronicle, some ice cream or a carton of smokes, small tin of aspirin. If it's an important medicine, he continued, I'll tell you or take it in my car.

He helped me to get bigger tips. Don't kill yourself. Just pedal on over at your regular speed. But, he advised, leaning in, when you get close, start pumping real hard. Throw down your bike and run up to the door and rap ten times, real hard. Yell out, DRUG STORE, DRUG STORE.
He smiled, You'll be panting, breathing hard and they'll tip better.

I tried it and it worked. I made twenty five cents an hour, ten bucks for a forty hour week. Mother insisted I give her two dollars of that and the government removed fifteen cents. Went to school full time, too. So, a twenty cent tip was a lot, to me.

I left work at ten and heard from Brother Gerry, who was in Mary June's class, and Mother, who knew the other Mom, how she did it.

When the bell rang at three, Mary June was ready. No books taken home; a special day.
She had waited and planned all year for the chance, knowing the boy's feet would still be tender and soft that first day of barefootin'.

Quickly, as Mrs. Nichols' dismissed class, Mary June was running full blast for the store. It was all over the neighborhood.

Girls and women seldom won anything then,

unlike today.

We did not get a Lady Governor in Texas last year, as many had wished, but hopes are still high for 2016, a Lady President for the Whole Danged Country.

Who knew, back then, at the Dawn of Time? I Am Woman; watch me kick some tail.

MY QUEST FOR SMALLER BREASTS!
Stephanie D. Lewis

"To change one's life: Start immediately. Do it
flamboyantly."
~William James

When I was 15, a boy inquired about going to the junior prom, never once taking his eyes off my enormous bosoms. I told him, "Oh yes, they'd be delighted to go." His baby blues widened as I continued, "They'll be ready by 7pm, but you need to return them safely back home and attached firmly to my torso by midnight." His eyes grew bigger than any saucers my breasts could ever fit into. "Or else...." I hesitated for dramatic effect, "they'll turn into pumpkins!" I couldn't resist. His eyes exploded.

After that incident, boys continued to never look into my eyes while speaking to me (but rather preferred to fix their stare a good 10 inches below), which prompted me to think about gluing those craft store Googly Eyes onto my blouse in strategic spots.

Hey listen to this . . . . . (God knows, I had to!)

"Where's your wheelbarrow?"

"Your cup runneth over!"

"Are melons in season?"

"Over the Shoulder Boulder Holder!"

"HELLO Dolly! Well, hello Dolly!" (sung to the Broadway musical tune).

There isn't a boob joke or cat-call I haven't heard before. In the past few months, I have used humor to help me lighten up with heavier issues than my breasts, so I'm going to give it a shot today – – being that I've had a breasted err, *vested* interest in the subject matter

When you're just 13 years-old and already making Dolly Parton look inadequate, you quickly learn that intelligent people who say, "Your bra size doesn't matter, only brain size matters," are just plain . . . Stupid. First of all, if you're big busted, you WILL be perceived as a bimbo, regardless of your IQ. Don't believe me? Try these 10 easy steps:

1. Fill two plastic bags with granulated sugar, each weighing 5.5 lbs and place them in your shirt (Yes, that was EACH.)

2. Go out tonight.

3. Oh, but first go bra shopping.

4. Bypass all the sweet, delicate, lacy little bralettes you see in the front of the store.

5. March up to a saleswoman and tell her you would like to (use the term "like to" loosely) try on a steel reinforced Chest of Armour in a size 38 Double . . . and then whisper the cup size.

6. Watch other women in the store turn to "envy" you. Slap forehead and say, "Darn! I just knew I shoulda ordered them in a smaller size when I was in that uterus."

7. Then try explaining to these other women about a) backaches b) shoulder pain c) not being able to sleep comfortably d) or exercise, e) combating extreme male crudeness f) your fear that someone will set a vase of flowers on your boobs, mistaking them for a fireplace mantle shelf. And g) well, "G" is your cup size.

8. Be prepared for these other women to shake their heads at your complete ungratefulness and proceed to bemoan the horrors of being a size A cup.

9. Nod politely and agree that yes, the grass is always greener. Or the bras are always better, on the other chest.

10. Go home and cry – – while fantasizing about carving pumpkins.

During high school, while girls on the Itty Bitty Titty Committee (remember that?) were saving up to buy a new set of wheels or a graduation trip to Hawaii, (in an "itty bitty, teeny weeny, yellow polka dot" *you know what,*) I was squirreling away my allowance for breast reduction surgery. But it wasn't looking good. My very protective father had already declared that, "No doctor was taking a scalpel to his small, little girl." Bless his heart with his choice of adjectives.

So I did what any typical female would do when something was "too large" on her body. I dieted to reduce their size. And I did lose weight, even though I didn't really need to. You can get quite disciplined when your only option of a swimsuit for the beach looks like something your grandmother would have worn. Circa 1929.

But this tactic only served to exacerbate my original problem, by making my waist smaller and accentuating a certain pair of...well let's just say I thought about making pumpkin pie all the time. It was time to try the opposite approach.

This time I ate a lot more food to attempt to camouflage them in excess weight. But they only inflated even more. While I was toying with the idea of trying a sharp pinprick, (would I zoom crazily airborne around the house like a balloon?) I happened to meet a nice boy. By this time I was exhausted from trying to change Mother Nature, (but you know what they always say, "No breast for the weary") and decided acceptance was my only answer.

Luckily, this boy was soft-spoken and at age 17, helped me cultivate somewhat of a sense of humor about them. He called me his "Little Treasure Chest." Compared to the names I heard walking by a construction site, this was definitely a breast of fresh air! One afternoon he leaned back comfortably against me, his head cradled between – well you know – singing along to that hit Police song, "Every breast you take....every move you make," when suddenly he announced that if he installed a couple of stereo speakers in them, he'd have himself a boob tube with Dolby Surround Sound headphones. That was it.

"You know what?" I asked. He waited with baited breast, I mean breath. "Give it a breast rest already! You and I are done." What a jerk, thinking he could just lie back and breast on his laurels. Ha – he wasn't the only one with good breast puns.

Besides, I couldn't have gone with him to my Senior Prom even if I wanted to. Why? Because Spaghetti Strap dresses were all the department stores sold. Could I wear that style?? Fat chance! Not even if it was supported by an entire bowl full of 100% durum wheat spaghetti straps!

Fast forward to age 18 and it was time to implement Plan B (and B was the exact letter I was going for with reduction surgery, by the way!) so I scheduled the operation. When the fateful morning arrived, I went to the hospital with just a bit of trepidation. In the operating room, the young, handsome, curly-haired Doctor came in and spoke to me, holding my hand while gazing deeply into my eyes, (a preview of what would be when I was finally smaller?) as he explained the exact procedure. I suppose he wanted to keep me abreast of everything that would occur.

He then exited out the door and I was alone with my itty-bitty thoughts. When the door opened next, a man walked in wearing surgical scrubs. I grew suspicious as he opened the front of my hospital gown and took out a black Sharpie pen.

Me: Wait a sec. Who are YOU?

Surgeon: *(drawing circles on my skin)* I'm the same guy who was here before. Only with a cap and mask. Why, who do you think I am?

Me: Oh I don't know. I thought maybe they were selling tickets out there for strange men to come inside and doodle on my breasts with magic markers.

Surgeon: Very funny. Have you considered Nursing in the future?

Me: Well, I get a little squeamish around blood. Why? Do you need an assistant?"

Surgeon: I meant breastfeeding. *(pause)* And you may not be able to. *(brightly)* So how do you feel about C's?

Me: I pride myself on being a straight A student, but I'll settle for a couple of B's.

Surgeon: A or B? But you'd be completely flat!?

Me: That's the idea. I wanna give people a craving for pumpkin pancakes.

When I woke up on that recovery table (even though I was in excruciating pain), – the first thing I did was reach down to feel the results, straight through the bandages. And in that moment, I knew . . . I would finally be able to say to my body, "Breast in Peace." Forever. Because I took charge and did something about my unhappiness!

THE DAY I KNEW
Edie Wyatt

*"All changes, even the most longed for, have their
melancholy; for what we leave behind us is
a part of ourselves; we must die to
one life before we can enter another."*
~Anatole France

I broke down into body-wrenching sobs as I stood at the kitchen sink washing a pot.

I broke down because of what I was thinking.

I was thinking, "One day, I don't think I'll be married to this man. I don't think I can stay married to this man."

It is so heart-breaking a thought, so terrifying a thought, so painfully sad a thought, that I couldn't stop the tears.

I've been holding these tears, these real, terrified, miserable, scared tears, for so long. They've been waiting for today, I think.

I tried to cover the sobs in the sound of the running water. But then I was crying so hard I couldn't see. I was about to drop the pot on the floor. I braced on the knob. The water turned off.

The dog heard me first. He yipped. Wondered what was wrong with me.

My husband paused the DVR. I tried to stop my pain from escaping, so messy, so loud. Too late.

He came over, placed his hands awkwardly on my shoulders as I faced away from him. His presence only made me cry harder. I'm going to have to leave you one day, I thought to myself.

My crying picked up at that hellish thought.
As I cried and cried, he eventually asked me what was wrong. How to say it?

"I don't know if I can do this," is what I choke out through tears and moans.

"I don't know either," he says. "Neither of us knows."

He's not understanding me. Of course he's not.

"I just don't know, I don't know if I can!" I'm crying into his chest now, simultaneously wanting to beat him and hug him. Instead I try to stem the flow of snot from my wet face.

85

He says, "We were fine, in a really good place, just last week. We'll be fine, we'll get through this."

"Well, that's not really true," I say. 'We' have not been in a good place in a long while. Since our travel abroad, since our return, when something broke, 'we' have not been in a good place. I have been fearful, worried, doubting.

"It's always there!" I cry. "It's always there for me, my fear that I can't do this with you!" It's such an enormous confession for me. I feel relieved for having said it. Lighter, already.

"Well, the threat of terrorism is always there…" He says this, incredibly, as he manages to simultaneously scoff at me and judge me and invalidate me yet again. This is his response to what, to me, are the most terrifying words one can ever really hear about themselves. That was his response.

Another nail in the coffin of this marriage. I heard the hammer swing down on that one.

His absurd immunity to my pain in that moment started to dry my tears. I felt baffled, disbelieving, amazed, angry at how he was reacting. Well, this is it, I thought to myself. This exact thing is why I can't. I moved back to the sink, resuming my abandoned pot-washing duty.

He stands there off to my left side. Hovering. Annoying.

"But...." He says. Still trying for logic, logic that fits in with his sense of himself and the world.

"But...what's wrong??"

You, I think. I take a deep breath. And speak the truth. "I'm not happy...at all." My tears resurface again. Pesky. I try to hold them in this time. I don't want him to see anymore.

I begin to fill the pot with water. Still, in all of this mess, it's time to cook the ravioli. As the water fills the pot, creeps up toward its rim, he speaks.

"That's enough."

Yes, I think. That's enough.

That was four years ago. Four years since I realized I would have to go.

And I did go.

It was the hardest thing I've ever done in my life, leaving my life. I walked away from nearly everything that I had ever been, everything that everyone thought I was. I walked away from my husband, my perfect-on-paper existence, my straightness. I left behind all of what I had worked toward for my entire life, because I finally, painfully, exhilaratingly realized that none of that work had actually been for me.

I had spent nearly 30 years doing exactly what was expected of me. I went to college, I found a boyfriend, I married him, I made a home, I got a dog. I was so locked in to being the good, nice, perfect girl that it took me 30 years of slowly, quietly, politely dying inside to realize that who I actually was looked nothing like the girl everyone knew.

I've learned that I am louder, darker, more cynical, more sensitive, more bawdy. I've learned that I can do things on my own, and that I want to. I've learned that I can handle hard times, handle anything. I've learned that I can love. I've learned that I am gay.

During the past four years, I have had some of the hardest moments of my life. I have been depressed. I have felt completely, terrifyingly alone. I have felt hopeless, and I have felt afraid.

But even when things were at their hardest, when I wasn't sure how I would make ends meet, when I feared that I'd never find love, when it seemed like no one understood, I still felt, underneath everything else, that I had done the right thing. In the midst of so much wrong, it still felt right. There was always a still relief nestled up against the pain.

That moment at the sink, the day I knew, was one of my lowest points. But it was also the moment of my release, and I have never looked back or felt more free.

LOSING MY VOICE

Kerri Lowe

*"Our lives begin to end the day we become
silent about the things that matter."*
~Martin Luther King Jr.

It dawned on me slowly, though I had been feeling it for weeks. My mind refused to take in a reality worse than a temporary pain. I have a cold and a sore throat, I thought. I'll get better soon.

But the reality was worse. The reality was that it hurt me to sing and I wasn't getting better anytime soon.

I was twenty-one years old and wild with thirst for life, for attention, for recognition as a gifted singer/songwriter. More than anything, I was thirsty for love, but only knew how to settle for lust.

I was on tour in New York City when it happened. New York was my former home that I had left just months before to record an album and start being a traveling songwriter in North Carolina. I was back in town to play my songs, see my friends, and seek out adventure before I forgot what the rush of the city felt like.

I'm not sure when the idea came over me. I had been seeing his work for over a year by that point. He was an artist, who drew nude faceless women with a talent I had never been able to pinpoint to an actual human. And certainly no human I had ever known personally. Artists were historically important dead men, not my acquaintances...but his drawings were exceptional works of eroticism, grit and beauty.

I wanted to be one of those girls. I wanted to push myself into something "I would never do." I was brought up to fear sex before marriage, but time and experience in the world silenced those fears just before I turned twenty. I was expanding my sensual self and finding pleasure based in respect and care, if not true love. It was a revelation to my traditional mind and I was ready to expand the boundaries of what I thought possible for myself even further.

I sent a message to the artist, who pushed me to summon the courage I tempted him with and go for it, pose for him. He would pay me like he did professional models and give me one of the paintings in exchange. This was a better deal than I had imagined, so we set a date.

The day I was supposed to model, I felt a sore throat coming on, probably a cold. I didn't want to chicken out, so I took some DayQuil and went to his apartment to be painted.

I took off my clothes and stood before his canvas. I was awkward and didn't know how to stand. I told him so and he asked if he could adjust me. I said yes and he approached slowly, put his hands on my sides and twisted my torso. I felt understandably nervous, but separated from the intimacy by pretending I was just a doll or a figurine. There was, after all, nothing sexual about the encounter. We talked intimately about my upbringing and feelings around sex, men, relationships, creativity. I felt safe, like I was with an interested but impartial judge. Being so exposed physically allowed me to tell him anything. I felt like I had nothing to protect.

Various poses took up the next forty minutes until we stopped for a break and to eat. We ordered food from the Chinese restaurant downstairs, ate together, and continued talking. He had poured some brandy for me when we started the session and I had taken a few sips. He was on a second drink, at least.

He asked if I wanted to do a more intense pose, with my legs open. I hesitated, thinking that it was a little much, but agreed. I'm here. I've gone this far. I might as well keep pushing myself, is how I thought about it.

He told me that the best way to do it was to get on his bed so he could draw from a chair, and only the slightest jolt of unease hit me. Small enough to ignore. I sat down on his bed and slowly eased my legs open, but my body rebelled. I started shaking uncontrollably. He touched my sternum and asked if I was alright.

"I don't know why I'm shaking," I said. I took a sip of brandy and said I'd be okay. "I'm fine."

He pulled a chair in front of me and started to draw. I continued to shake as he leaned in and studied me intently. I had never been so exposed to anyone in my life. Bizarre. I closed my eyes. He finished a drawing and showed it to me.

He wanted to do another and asked if he could adjust my leg. I said "Okay," and felt his hand on my calf pulling me closer, spreading my legs farther. Suddenly I felt his mouth on me and jerked back into the fetal position.

I was frozen. Unable to move or speak. Finally, I said, "I should go," and got up to put on my clothes. I dressed as fast as I could and started for the door, but he held me back.

"Don't leave!" he said. "Talk to me. Hit me. Say something."

It took me too long to form words, but finally a question escaped. "What were you thinking?"

"I wasn't thinking. I just...blacked out. I don't know what happened. I'm sorry."

He was getting upset, starting to cry even - so I hugged him and told him it was okay. I tried to leave again and he wanted me to stay, try again, but I knew better than that. He followed me partway down the stairs.

"You'll hate me now!" he said. "You'll hate art." And then, "I was supposed to pay you!"

I ran out the door and flung myself around the corner before breaking down sobbing. I called a guy I knew who lived nearby, who walked me around and held my hand as I told him what happened.

I didn't go to the police. I didn't know what to do. I didn't want to ruin his life if it was an accident, but I also knew that people who did things like that could be manipulative. What if the tears were just a show? What if I was putting other girls in danger by not saying anything? I sent emails to the girls I knew who had also modeled for him or had thought about it. I told them what happened to me, asked if they had experienced anything bad, and encouraged them to tell other women to stay away from him.

About a month later, it hit me. My throat had been hurting since the day I modeled for him. I assumed I was just sick, that I kept getting this cold over and over again, but I knew I wasn't sick any longer. This was strange. And it hurt most when I tried to sing.

I got scared that I had developed vocal nodules, or something worse, from singing while I was sick. I did a few shows while my throat was sore because I had no choice, even though I knew it was unhealthy to do so. I gave myself panic attacks obsessing about what I had done to my voice. Finally, I went to the doctor. He looked at my vocal cords and said there were no nodules, but a lot of redness. It looked like I had acid reflux.

I told the doctor that I had been on and off bulimic since I was fifteen and we agreed that this must be the reason. I told him that the last few years, I wasn't actually making myself throwing up, it had just become a reflex. I told him I thought I could stop it on my own. He put me on a pill that kept my stomach from producing acid so my throat could heal itself and not get worse.

I felt like the ultimate failure. I had ruined my career and my life with my eating disorder. I could no longer do the thing that meant the most to me. It was like an Olympic sprinter breaking their leg, with no guarantee that it would ever be strong enough to run on again. What I didn't realize, was that the eating disorder was only part of my illness. The other cause couldn't be found by an ear, nose, and throat doctor.

After a year and a half of being unable to consistently sing without pain, I started to realize that my problem was mental and emotional as well as physical. I traced the timing of my vocal loss back to the sexual assault and I realized something. By keeping my assault a secret, I had silenced myself. I was afraid to speak. Maybe my body manifested that *literally* into being unable to sing.

I read everything I could get my hands on about healing physical symptoms through becoming more mentally and emotionally healthy. I read about chronic illnesses that people overcame with their minds, simply by believing they could. I started to see a therapist to whom I could tell my story. I read about narrative medicine and the power of the stories you tell about yourself – how changing those stories can change your physical reality. I realized that in order to heal my voice, I was going to need to tell the truth about what happened to me.

I began writing a one-woman show, not only about that experience, but about my entire coming-of-age story and everything that led to that moment. I got the okay to sing from the doctor, who told me the redness was gone from my vocal cords. I forced myself to sing a little bit everyday and to learn techniques that would reduce tension and fear around singing. Most importantly, I gave voice to the thing in my past I was most scared and ashamed of. After almost a year of this work, I performed my show without vocal pain and have been singing again without fear.

Losing my voice was the hardest challenge I ever faced, but going through that experience taught me to forgive myself, tell the truth and never give up. It taught me I must recognize and process my feelings rather than ignoring them. I often comfort myself with some words from the famous songwriter and poet, Leonard Cohen. He said, "There's a crack in everything, that's how the light gets in." I know now that when I let the light come into my broken places, I find I have nothing to hide.

ENDING THE AFFAIR
Eileen Goddard

*"The journey of a thousand miles
begins with a single step."*
~Lao Tzu

I smoked my first cigarette when I was 16 years old. I had stolen it from the carton of Marlboros that my dad kept in the laundry room, which I had been eyeing with curiosity for weeks. One day, I finally snuck out a single cigarette and drove myself to the local park. It was a small town, so I climbed inside a grove of bushes, just in case someone I knew walked by. It took me three matches to get the cigarette lit, and I remember the dry choking as smoke first entered my lungs. I barely took three puffs before stubbing it out in the dirt. I couldn't believe that anyone actually did this thing on purpose. I drove home, disgusted with myself, and washed my hands over and over, trying to take away the smell.

I smoked my second cigarette a year later, at the Dixie Classic Fair. I was standing in a circle with friends, and when someone passed around a pack of Camels, I took one. As I inhaled, my legs went weak, and my head euphorically dizzy. It was the closest thing to being high I'd ever felt, and it felt good. Good enough that I wanted to feel that way again. Two days later, I bought my first pack at the gas station by school that didn't check ID's.

I loved smoking right away - there was something exciting, defiant, and a little bit dangerous about it. Although looking back, smoking really wasn't so unusual or taboo where I grew up. Living twenty minutes away from R.J. Reynolds meant that there were Kool and Joe Camel billboards everywhere, and cigarettes were plentiful and cheap. There were sprawling green tobacco fields just down the road from the house where I grew up. But smoking cigarettes wasn't just about those things - it was about me, too, about how I have the thing inside me that some people call an "addictive personality." Different addictions run through my family history, and I can feel that potential for addiction inside myself too. I was never someone who could smoke "one cigarette." I smoked for nine years, and there was hardly a day in those years when I didn't smoke a full pack.

I smoked my last cigarette on November 20, 2010. I had recently read *The Easy Way to Stop Smoking* by Allen Carr, and reading that book had shifted something inside me. For the first time in nearly a decade, I knew that I wanted to quit. I was so naïve - I still thought that I only smoked because it was something I "enjoyed" doing, and I honestly thought that quitting would be easy. I had no idea how dependent, how addicted I had become.

I still couldn't see the way cigarettes limited me - how while hanging out with friends, I was always plotting my next escape outside for a smoke. How at the airport, I risked missing connecting flights, just for the chance to take a couple of drags. My daily life revolved around cigarettes - buying them, worrying about when and where I'd be able to smoke them, smoking them, and then later, buying more.

More than four years later, I can still say with absolute certainty that quitting smoking is the hardest thing I have ever done.

The 48 hours after my final cigarette were a waking nightmare. I felt inhuman. Every pore of my body screamed constantly for a cigarette. My head throbbed. I felt insane. Every minute stretched into infinity - an hour felt like days. For anyone who has never been addicted to anything, withdrawal is a difficult sensation to explain. It's an extreme claustrophobia that descends over you, taking over every sense and every thought - there are no real thoughts anymore, only the incessant, constant desire for a cigarette in your head.

I had to work every day that first week, and I remember running frantically at one point to the herb shop across the street. I basically screamed in the woman's face, "I JUST QUIT SMOKING - PLEASE HELP ME!" She sold me a bottle of licorice tincture, which tasted awful, but I took frantic little shots of it straight out of the dropper a couple of times an hour every day that week.

It got better, of course. Slowly, I relearned how to live each day without cigarettes, and in the end, my life and my health is much better for the transformation. I can easily say now that I don't miss smoking anymore. But it took awhile - it was only after three years of having quit that I finally stopped wishing for a cigarette sometimes after a couple of glasses of wine, that I finally stopped having the same recurring smoking dreams every week.

Now I realize how important it was for me to go through the nightmarish process of quitting - the fact that it was so incredibly difficult is the biggest reason why I never started smoking again.

Because starting again is easy - tobacco is legal, and for somewhere between $5-$15, you can buy a pack or a pouch of it almost anywhere in the world. Since the day I quit, I have consumed tobacco products exactly twice.

The first time, I smoked part of a cigar at a wedding, and the second time, I smoked a few puffs of a clove cigarette with a friend while my boyfriend was out of town. Both of those times were turning points in which I almost went back to smoking. Even after ingesting just the smallest amount of tobacco, I would crave cigarettes all over again for weeks.

The last time, when I smoked the clove, was what finally got me "over" smoking for good. Because honestly, that clove was delicious. I felt high again, just like I had at the Dixic Classic Fair when I was 17. My friend left me two more clove cigarettes on my coffee table "for later," and when I woke up the next morning and saw them lying there, I briefly entertained the idea of smoking them. Instead, I tore them up and threw them in the trash can while thinking, "No way, I'm not doing this again."

But life is long, and the present moment is what's important. Although I feel confident that I will never smoke a cigarette again, you just can't predict the future. What I do know is that I am grateful to have learned how to live happily without cigarettes. I've learned that I am both stronger and more human than I ever realized, and both of these things are good.

Although I identify myself as a non-smoker all the time now, that's not completely true; I'm an ex-smoker now, and I'm an ex-smoker always. I hope that I never forget my own history, or my ability to relate to and help other people struggling with - and overcoming - addictions of their own.

Pivotal Moments

"Experience is merely the name we give our mistakes."

- Oscar Wilde

A RABBI WITH PURPLE HAIR
Rebecca W. Sirbu

"To be yourself in a world that is constantly trying to make you something else is the greatest accomplishment."
~Ralph Waldo Emerson

I was hip for a week. For one week, I had a stripe of purple hair mixed in with my usual brown shiny locks. I loved it! I felt bolder, braver, and more fun. Most of all, it just made me smile to see it in the mirror.

Frankly, I needed to smile. A couple of weeks earlier, a good friend died of aggressive breast cancer. Her untimely death woke me up. I understood in a new way how fragile and short life is. It is a cliché that we need to live life as fully as possible while we have it—but it is true. We do.

My friend lived life loud, literally. She had a big presence and a booming voice. You always knew when she was in the room. She embraced all things silly and fun, and let you know you were missing out if you did not participate.

In the midst of my sadness, I realized that I needed more fun in my life. I was missing out on some things. Since adolescence, I have wanted to dye my hair some funky color, purple, blue, hot pink. Yet, I never did. I felt the time had arrived.

So, I walked in to a hair salon and asked to dye my hair. The hair stylist suggested I go an easier route and put in a pre-dyed hair extension. She explained that it would last a month or two and was cheaper and less complicated than dye. Five minutes later I had purple hair!

I felt liberated. Finally, my inner punk was on full display.

I texted friends and posted a picture on Facebook. The outpouring of joy and support was immediate. My favorite Facebook comment was   "Ok, You're my rabbi." I was further astounded by the number of women who told me that they were jealous, that they wanted to be that brave, that they wanted to do it too!

Sadly, a week later, my purple hair extension silently slipped out of my hair. Apparently, my never before dyed or processed hair was too "healthy and silky" to firmly hold it in place. If only I had been more of a rebel when I was younger…

I would have liked it to last longer; however, the week with purple hair was a revelation. I learned several things. Many, many women like me are putting off being their whole selves, or true selves. I was astounded by the number of women who shared with me how they wanted to do something similar, yet something was holding them back.

As a rabbi, I encourage others to be their best selves, to bring their dreams and aspirations into reality. So if you have something you want to do, be it dying your hair a funky color, or changing a major part of your life — just do it! Life is short, if you let your fears and doubts hold you back from being who you want to be and achieving what you want, then you will miss out on something precious.

I also learned that people are far less judgmental than you think when you present yourself strongly and confidently. When people asked why I had purple in my hair, I answered honestly that I needed a little fun in my life. I got smiles and nods in return.

I love doing out-of-the-box things as a rabbi. I have never fit into boxes very well. My sense is that most of us don't. So watch out! The purple hair is likely to come back. Or I may try something else…I am open to ideas. How else can I express my inner punk?

This article was reprinted with permission from the Rabbis Without Borders blog of MyJewishLearning.com, a website devoted to pluralistic Jewish information and engagement.

MY FRIENDLY CARJACKING
Shannon Whitten

"Charity begin at home, and justice begins next door."
~Charles Dickens

Why is this happening and why is this man jumping into my front seat? These were just a few of the thoughts racing through my brain at the gas station on North Avenue. Did he have a gun, or a knife under his generic grey sweatsuit? I'm still not sure, but the threat was palpable.

He announced boldly that his son was hospitalized at Crawford Long around the corner and he needed money for his family to eat. I'm a nurse and this seemed plausible, a family caught off guard with a sick child and a wallet at home on the coffee table. I was sure he couldn't be lying, even with him holding me at weapon point.

He asked for my money, but I had none. I was in grad school so I offered my credit cards. He insisted I go to an ATM, but when I told him I had none of my PIN numbers he further insisted I go to the Kroger and use my debit for a cash return.

I followed his instructions, plotting my escape the entire time. All the while, me making "I'm In Danger" faces at the customers in the store. Do I scream, do I turn into Wonder Woman, do I tell the cashier to call for help by passing her a slip of paper? No, I do none of these, holding out hope that maybe humanity is good and maybe my polite kidnapper is a decent human being, despite the obvious.

My lack of panic was surprising, as I am not a 'keep calm in the storm' kind of person. I drove him back to the point of origin because he asked me to do this for him. After all, his family was waiting. As he fled on foot, I was left sitting alone in my thoughts, the hot tears filled my face and I started shaking violently as I finally came to terms and realized this was a serious. This carjacking, while a surreal adventure at the time, could have stolen my life away.

I continued contemplating his story for five minutes until my husband called asking if I was alright. How could he possibly have known that I wasn't? He proceeded that the "police" called needing my credit card Pin numbers and they had informed him that I had been carjacked.

Yes, no more fantasizing about this man in my car as a decent human being. I had my answer. I had the truth and needed the truth to resolve this situation - to get angry and to move forward and to forgive. I can now look back on this and joke a bit, but I still really deep down wish my original assessment of this man was truth, and that he had done this out of desperation instead of the criminal act it really was.

THE FARMHOUSE

Kathy Sechrist

"The boundaries which divide Life from Death are at best shadowy and vague. Who shall say where the one ends, and where the other begins?"
~Edgar Allan Poe

Sliding into the cold leather seats, a chill found it's way into my wool coat, bringing with it a longing for the warm bed I begrudgingly left just 30 minutes ago. It was Tuesday, which meant leaving the house early to get to the office in time for the sales meeting at 8:00am. As the office manager of a popular real estate office on the island, I facilitated the meeting and afterward left with the Realtors to view the new weekly listings, taking notes and pictures for marketing purposes.

A ten minute drive to work always made me feel blessed to live on Whidbey Island, with it's forests, pastoral farmland and light traffic. This particular morning was typical November, with fog shrouding the barely visible trees and mist just light enough to cover the windshield, but not enough to engage the automatic wipers. The gray, blurred world seemed surreal. I shuddered with an eerie feeling it was an omen of something to come.

The meeting lasted about an hour, after which we decided to grab one more cup of hot coffee for warmth and one more donut for fortitude before venturing out. As the others decided who was driving, I grabbed the camera and notepad and found an empty seat in Janet's van. We made our way up and down the island while a few complained about the weather, leaving the rest of us quiet, lost in our thoughts.

The last house on our viewing schedule was an old 1800 vintage farmhouse that belonged to one of Central Whidbey's pioneering families. Generations lived and farmed and raised their families in that house. A heaviness surrounded me. Another change in our safe, comfortable world - where everyone knows everyone else - was represented in the sale of that house.

Janet turned the van into the long, unpaved drive leading to the house. A lone tree stood in front, bare with the exception of one leaf clinging to a limb, soggy from the mist in the air. Stepping out of the van, I noticed the leaf falling to the ground, quietly and without ceremony. With a sense of foreboding, I stood in the drive taking pictures of the property. From the outside, the house looked tall and thin, with the siding showing the results of years of prairie wind carrying topsoil with it, stripping the paint away. The once well-tended flower garden had been overtaken by weeds and climber vines wound around the posts that held the roof over the front porch.

I gasped in surprise as my foot almost went through the rotted wood of the bottom stair of the porch. Gingerly, I made my way up to the front door to catch up to the others. Standing in front of the open door, a wispy figure of a woman flickered into view and disappeared as quickly as she appeared. A shiver curled through the hairs on the back of my neck then cascaded down my spine. It was all I could do to not turn around and run back to the van. I looked at the others to see what their reaction was, but it didn't seem as if they saw the woman. Frightened and confused, I looked around again. She was gone.

Chiding myself for being over dramatic, I stepped into the room, which by my guess was the parlor. It was dull and smelt of dust mixed with old age. The wallpaper was peeling off the walls, and the floorboards creaked with each step. I noticed a picture of a woman hanging a little lopsided on one of the walls near the parlor stove. As I peered closer, I recognized her as the woman I had seen when I walked into the room. She wore a black, high-collared dress with a white lace collar, and her gray hair was pulled back into a tight bun. My hand immediately covered my mouth to stop the scream building in my throat as her sad eyes held mine captive.

In a panic, I quickly spun around and, realizing I was alone in the room, hurried to the kitchen to join the others. In a shaky voice, I asked if anyone had seen anything weird; they all looked at me as if I had lost it. A sinking feeling came over me when I remembered I hadn't taken any pictures yet. With shaky hands I quickly took few of the parlor and kitchen while the others climbed the narrow wooden staircase to the second floor, where the bedrooms were.

Finished with taking pictures of the downstairs, I stood at the bottom of the stairs the others had just climbed. With a sense of dread I slowly made my way up when all of a sudden a freezing blast of air blew past me from behind and as soon as I felt it, it was gone. I clutched the banister and hurried up the stairs frustrated that my imagination had run away with me yet again.

The feeling of dread remained as I began taking notes and pictures of the first two bedrooms. The third bedroom was the closest to the top of the stairs. Looking up from my notes, I took one step inside to the now familiar cold blast of air I had felt coming up the stairs. My scream froze when I saw her standing by the window, framed by tattered curtains. As she turned to look at me, I felt rather than saw her profound sense of sadness and heartbreak. I couldn't move; I was frozen in time with her spirit. Suddenly, she turned back to gaze out the window.

Not understanding why, I swallowed back tears, slowly backed out of the room and made my way down the stairs, carrying with me her sadness and heartbreak. The others were already getting settled in the van, and as I looked around the rooms one last time my earlier fear was replaced with a sadness I could not explain. Not to myself, not to anyone.

As we drove back down that long driveway, I turned, and through the rear window I saw her peering through the flimsy curtains, watching us leave. Her sadness and heartache stayed with me on the short drive back to the office. Quickly I downloaded the pictures from the camera and an icy chill went up my spine when, in the picture of the bedroom, she was there, a ghostly figure standing by the window. I didn't use the picture to market the house, but kept it for years and wondered if she would ever find what she was looking out the window for.

The house eventually sold to a family with young children. They have renovated it, trimmed back the climbing vines and planted colorful flowers in the garden that border the porch. I pass by it on my way home sometimes, and when I do I always slow down and look to see if she is there, standing in the window. I haven't seen her since the family moved in; perhaps her spirit is now at peace.

Have you ever had a paranormal experience?

I AM HERE

Anna Delamerced

"Wherever there is a human being, there is an opportunity for a kindness."
~Seneca

The room is empty, save for a small group of students crouched at their computers in the corner, a young man lunching at a table near the exit, and me.

The yellowed bulbs emit a glow, a dim one, as if holding on for dear life, clinging to the last bit of energy warranted to their lifetime. A mixture of dining and bistro tables dot the former bar-turned-haven for late lunchers and procrastinators like me.

I sit, furiously typing away at my keyboard, partly raging at myself for not finishing my chemistry lab report earlier, partly raging at the world for the existence of said chemistry lab reports. The half-eaten turkey sandwich sits an arm's length away from me as my stomach growls, piercing the otherwise quiet basement of the student center. I look up, sheepishly, wondering if anyone heard.

My eyes meet an elderly woman who crosses the threshold and into the space, her eyes searching for an empty chair, and her feet shuffling across the linoleum floor once she finds one, a table away from me.

As if a pebble collapsing into a pond, her body sinks into the chair, elbows propped, head slumped into her hands. For a few minutes, she just lies there in that state of stillness.

The phone in my pocket buzzes, reminding me that I have to embark for lab soon, across campus. One more question to answer, then I can leave.

But before I can return my eyes to the computer screen, my gaze catches the elderly woman yet again. Her eyes are pools of gray, as if cloths of melancholy were covering her irises. Weathered yet resilient, her fingers massage the tiny waves of creases on her forehead. In her palms lays a book, leather-bound, worn, yet she clutches it with the utmost sincerity and regard.

I don't know what it is, but something is stirring in the depths of my inmost being, depths I knew not of until now. She must have been on a short break from working at the cafe on the floor above. She keeps trying to iron out her collar, the Brown Dining Services emblem stitched on her front pocket of her green polo shirt. I can tell something is bothering her. I want to ask, yet am too afraid to trek across the unsaid divide between youth and elderly, between student and staff, between strangers.

And yet, the fibers of my soul are tugged, revealing to me a person in need of grace, in need of a listening heart, in need of outstretched hands.

Moments come when you reach a crossroad, and you have been given the will to decide for yourself which direction you want to take. I am not the most outspoken, nor the most outgoing. I am not the bravest, nor the boldest. Yet in that moment, I decided what path I wanted to take.

I lift myself out of my seat and walk over to her table. I am about to apologize bumblingly for my intrusion, but when I see her eyes, tired, longing for hope, I simply ask:

"May I pray with you?"

A spark lit up as she smiles and nods. Surprised, yet joyful, I accept her invitation to sit. I bend my head, and stretch open my heart to pray. For strength, for understanding, for steadfast hope when waters rise.

I knew not exactly why I was doing this, nor did I know exactly what to pray for. But then she tells me that this prayer time was a blessing from heaven. Her husband is ill and in the hospital. He had just suffered a stroke earlier that week, so she has been reading a book of prayers in search for answers and clarity and peace. This prayer with me, though unexpected, came at the right time. It was something in which she rejoiced.

We begin talking. She is from Cape Verde; English is her second language. Though we come from different generations and different geographies, knowing that we are here at the right time in the right place transcends fear of judgment.

As I finish praying, I glance up and see tears beginning to well in her eyes, dancing down her cheek. I could tell these tears were a mixture of pain and joy. Pain, for her husband's suffering. Yet joy, in knowing that she was not alone. In that moment, all I can do is stretch out my hands, hold hers in mine, and let her know that I am here, for her.

Our lives intertwine with purpose, our encounter on this day written in the heavens long before we both were born. Love for a fellow human casts out fear, if you let it.

Everyday Heroes

"Do not go where the path may lead;
go instead where there is no path
and leave a trail."

- Ralph Waldo Emerson

DROWNING

Kevin Baker

"There are dark shadows on the earth, but its lights are stronger in the contrast."
~*Charles Dickens*

One fine summer's day, two friends and I were partying a little down by the lake, lazing about in the sun and swimming. We were sitting on the end of the jetty, drinking beer, and joking around. Every now and then we would jump into the cool, clear lake, splash around a while, then swim to the shallows and get back on the jetty.

After one of these cool-off swims I was second out of the water. As I walked back onto the jetty, I noticed number three was not present. Number one had walked to the car to fetch something, so I looked around for number three. Nowhere. I thought maybe he was playing a trick by hiding under the jetty or something, so I walked out to the end and peered over the edge. I looked into the water just in time to see him sinking slowly away into the depths. It was like that scene in the movie "Titanic", near the end, where Jack sinks slowly out of sight.

I'll never forget his face - he was looking up through the water at me and grinning, but it was such a strange grin, I knew something was seriously wrong. In one of those big moments in life that only last a split-second, but everything seems to go in slow-motion. I puzzled through what his look meant, and then it struck me: "He's drowning!"

I fell on the jetty, plunging my arm into the water and grabbed his hand just in time, while shouting for help. Number one came running, as did a paramedic who happened to be picnicking nearby and who had heard my shout for help. The three of us hauled the half-drowned number three up onto the jetty. He was already turning blue and had stopped breathing - his lungs full of water - but the paramedic did some CPR for a minute or so until number three spewed up a bucketful of water, coughed and started breathing again.

Wow! He was going to be ok. That was the end of our fun that day, but the strangest thing was that he never thanked me for saving his life. It all happened many years ago, and I've never seen him since, but I did hear a week or so later that he had made a full recovery. I also heard that he had previously been diagnosed with clinical depression, and had once tried to take his own life. Maybe I got in his way that day.

THE REAL GIVER
Traci O'Connell

"A teacher affects eternity;
he can never tell where his influence stops."
~Henry Adams

I was stashing files and clearing off my desk, when his silhouette filled the open classroom door.

"I just came to say goodbye," he said and moved into the empty classroom.

Evan had just come off the football field, dressed in his navy blue cap and gown, where the seniors had just finished graduation practice.

"Hey, Evan," I said, genuinely happy to see him. "I'm glad you came. Did they tell you I was looking for you?"

"Ya," he smiled and looked down, a boyish shyness clinging to him on his final day of high school.

"I have something for you," I said, and reached into my bag to hand him a copy of *The Giver*.

He looked to the side, clearly emotional. "Wow. Thank you, so much." His wide eyes beamed as he scanned the cover. "This is the best book I've ever read. It's nice to have my own copy."

I didn't usually give gifts to students, but some classes are special, and the Class of 1998 was extraordinary. So many of them sparkled, and not because they were all exceptionally smart. Some were brighter than others, but they all tried. They all pictured themselves being better than the place where they started, and they came into my class like a group of old friends ready to connect.

We first met when they were squirrely tenth graders. I taught in a Los Angeles magnet school where our student population was limited and our staff small, so I always taught all of the sophomores and seniors. In 1998, I looked forward to my Honors Advanced Comp class every day. I wanted them ready for college, and they were hungry. Together we discussed Chaucer's satirical wit and debated Hamlet's sanity. We wrote and wrote. They worked hard for me, but a few of them broke my heart; like Evan.

When you have the same kids for two years, you get to know them pretty well, and because Evan was a sweet, hard-worker, admired as the campus math whiz, he stood out right away. But he carried a secret. He entered school at seven, speaking only Spanish, and moved ten times during his elementary years, often skipping months of school during relocations. So much disruption in the continuity of his instruction caused serious gaps in his reading skills.

As a tenth grader, it was immediately apparent to me that he struggled to read. Though he faked his way through class discussions, his writing revealed that the material we read was too advanced for his comprehension level. Because he was in an accelerated program, and excelled in math, he was unlikely to qualify for intervention - it was the unfortunate reality of being part of a vast bureaucratic system I couldn't control. Evan worked hard to conceal his weakness. I did what I could to help him, but it wasn't enough. I never put Evan in an awkward position, but he often sat at his desk with fear in his eyes. I harbored my own fear when I thought of him; how could I send this kid to college, knowing he has never completed a book, knowing he had never experienced the joy of reading?

Near the end of the spring semester, we delved into *1984*, and class discussion was lively. Evan excitedly considered the parallels between Orwell's grim predictions and the reality of post-1984 America. After two years of watching him shy away from discussions, he suddenly came alive, but I knew from his written work that while he liked the ideas of the book, he wasn't reading the text. Then, suddenly, I realized I could give Evan a gift.

Several days later, I asked him to stay after class and handed him a school copy of *The Giver* with a work packet I created. I encouraged him to continue participating in class discussions about 1984, but I wanted him to read *The Giver*. I explained the themes of both books were similar, but I felt he would enjoy reading *The Giver* more. He would write a paper on *The Giver* and take tests on *The Giver*, and no one else needed to know that his work differed from the group.

He agreed and took the book, looking a little scared separating from the safety of the group. What he didn't know was while *1984* is written at an eleventh-grade level, *The Giver* is written at a sixth-grade level. What I didn't know was how much the right book could bring a child alive. By the third day into *The Giver*, Evan was on fire during class discussions. He openly made comparisons between *1984* and *The Giver*, sparking an interest in both books in other students and taking class conversations in directions that were surprising and thoughtful. He sometimes popped into class a few minutes early to talk about what he had read on previous nights. He eagerly completed the work packet and wrote the best paper I had ever seen from him.

Being able to put an A on his paper was one of my favorite teaching moments.

"You're going tonight, right?" he asked tucking the book into his back pocket.

"Of course! Wouldn't miss it, but, be warned; I might cry." He laughed, and I gave him a hug in case we didn't see each other in the melee of 600 kids tossing caps into the air. Then he walked into the June sun. I stifled tears and got back to work. A few minutes later, his freckled face peeked around my door.

"You're back," I said looking up.

"I just want you to know this is the first book I've ever read," he said, waving *The Giver* in his hand.

"I know." The look we exchanged communicated more than we'd ever spoken aloud.

"I'll take good care of it," and he tucked it away again. "Thank you so much. Really," he said and was gone.

I became a teacher because I loved books and writing. I didn't know how much I would love the kids. Thank you so much, Evan. Really.

THE EPISTLE OF PETER
Clara Klein

"What is right to be done cannot be done too soon."
~Jane Austen

Summer vacation in Wisconsin was the time for getting outside, relaxing and having fun. It signified freedom – for kids, freedom from school, and for adults, freedom from cabin fever. It was the 1960's. My siblings and I enjoyed an idyllic childhood in a suburb outside of Milwaukee, where it was green and beautiful. In those early Baby Boomer days, suburbs were a newly popular idea. We grew up with amenities a lot of families did not have and one of them was a built-in swimming pool. All seven siblings spent a good part of their time outdoors in the huge yard we had. We were outside summer and winter, sharing picnics and playing games. Summer memories included sitting on a swing under a huge maple tree, watching our dad barbeque, and singing the songs of the sixties. It seemed like the perfect dream. But one day, the dream turned into a nightmare. That was the day I grew up.

I was the youngest of the family. I took that role from my brother Peter, who was sibling number six in an eventual line of seven. Peter was not that close to me. I suspected he was jealous of me because he was no longer the baby of the family, a position he had secured for four and a half years. Peter tormented me whenever he could, and I saw him as an adolescent ogre. He was constantly being nasty to me, ditching me, making fun of me, and getting me into trouble. I guess it was the trickle-down effect: the older siblings picked on him, and the only one left for him to pick on was me. Once I was a witness to the three older brothers beating him up until his nose bled.

The oldest brother was out of the house when I was only in the first grade. That's how I remember the vacating of the house – by what grade I was in. The oldest sister left when I was in third grade, the next when I was in fifth, and so on. By the time I was thirteen, and just out of the eighth grade, it was only Peter and I in the house with our parents. And he was graduating from high school and would soon be off on his own as well.

It was a summer morning like any other. It was

133

quiet in the house. The only ones home were my mom, Peter and me. Mom and I were up early. She was going about taking care of the house and I was wandering about, thinking about going outside. As I stared out the patio door that led to the pool, I noticed something strange. There was a pile of little clothes on the concrete patio. That's funny, I thought, I didn't play with dolls anymore, so they couldn't be something I left lying around.

Then I looked beyond to the pool and there was an awful sight. A baby – in fact, it almost looked like a doll – was floating face down in the pool. I couldn't believe what I was seeing. Was I dreaming? It took me a moment to react, then I screamed. I ran upstairs to my mom. "Oh, what is it?" she asked sarcastically, "a dead body?"

"Yes," I said meekly. "Yes, it is." I pointed outside and my mom placated me by looking out at the pool. Then she just screamed and screamed. This woke Peter up from a deep sleep and I saw him barrel down the stairs from his bedroom in his underwear. "What's going on?" Both my mom and I stammered out the words – baby – pool – drowned.

Peter, unabashed by his appearance, bolted out the back door and into the pool in a matter of seconds. He grabbed that baby and had it out on the patio, lying on its back in no time. Then he pumped the little chest and tried to resuscitate her.

It worked, and soon the baby was coughing up all this water. Mom wrapped the little one with one of our beach towels and we tried to calm her. In all the commotion, the police and an ambulance were called and we related the story. Somehow the baby's family showed up, but I really don't know what they did next. Later we found out second-hand that the child was fine and there were no complications.

Peter was written up in the paper as a local hero, and given a citizenship award. I saw a different side of my obnoxious brother that day. It showed me that even the most unlikely person can become a hero.

Peter died suddenly in 2000, five days before his 46th birthday, due to an aortic aneurysm. I believe he left an epistle for us.

Throughout his adult life, he would make a lot of bad decisions. He even called himself the black sheep of the family. Many times we never even knew where he was living. We wouldn't hear anything for months at a time, and then all of a sudden he would show up at a brother's, sister's, or cousin's house to stay for a while. He crisscrossed the country, living one time on the east coast, and another time on the west. We knew he did some freelance photography, but weren't sure that he was supporting himself that way.

Sometimes stories filtered their way back to us about Peter having financial or other troubles. He also seemed to avoid talking to our parents, probably afraid of how they'd react.

Sometimes when I think of Peter, I get angry for the bad memories he left. But then I remember the time he was a hero and chastise myself to remember the good stuff. Even though he had trouble in his lifetime, Peter had a desire to be good in his heart. His memory reminds us that in spite of our wrongdoings, we can balance karma in our lives by doing something good. With luck, most of us have a saving grace.

You never know, life can be over without any warning, so it's good to ask yourself, will there be a moment in your life that will outweigh anything bad you've done? Perhaps now is the time to create it.

WOUNDED AND VULNERABLE
Sidney Bending

"The cure for all the ills and wrongs, the cares, the sorrows,
and the crimes of humanity, all lie in the one word 'love.'
It is the divine vitality that everywhere
produces and restores life."
~Lydia M. Child

In those days, they gutted you – uterus, fibroids, fallopian tubes, ovaries – "none of these are necessary." I had a scar as big as two eyebrows – frowning. Nowadays, there are more civilized options.

They said it takes over a year to recuperate from a hysterectomy. It had only been a week.

I couldn't walk fast or far, but wanted to see the neighborhood gardens. My mother had taken me in to recuperate at her house, my childhood home.

"Look at those purple clematis beside the Jensen's garage. They grow bigger every year. Mrs. McIver had to take out that bush but replaced it with these roses. Breathe in."

We inched our way around the block arm-in-arm.

By the lane, a buzz saw buzzed and somebody hammered the side of a house. He didn't notice that his dog was out of the yard, barking viciously. Although we could hardly have looked threatening, the large German Shepherd charged at us with teeth snarling.

My instinct was to curl into myself – double over to protect what was left of my internal organs. But my mother was magnificent. She stomped on the pavement in front of me. A deep voice came out of her that I'd never heard before – a grisly growl.

"Get out of here! Get now! Get!" She shook her fist in the air brandishing nothing but resolve.

He yelped, crouched, turned tail and ran.

My mother saved me. Her 'momma-bear' instincts rose up. Even in her 70's, she was fierce.

To commemorate her rescue, I bought a little thank you gift for her crystal collection – a transparent teddy bear with a coloured center – the purple heart for bravery.

Moments of Gratitude

"Gratitude is the sign of noble souls."

– Aesop

GUARDING LIFE
Robin Botie

"Reflect upon your present blessings, of which every man has plenty; not on your past misfortunes, of which all men have some."
~Charles Dickens

"You don't magically recover in a year's time," says Meg, my social worker who still keeps tabs on me eighteen months after The Three Years I lived in the trenches of a war on cancer.

"But I'm tired of being accident-prone and making poor choices. Forgetting. Falling. Losing things. Breaking things," I tell her. "Missing appointments was something someone else always did. My eyes are cried bloodshot. I can't even dress myself right. I used to be a teacher. I was a lifeguard. I took care of other people's children. Except for childbirth, I was never in a hospital for my own care until this past year. Now I've broken a wrist, my nose and two toes. I had vertigo last week. And Lyme disease."

"Take care of yourself," Meg says.

And I think, Yeah, I'm my own lifeguard now. Only there's nothing and no one left to guard. And I can't even pull myself up out of the dark depths of despair.

Driving home shortly after, a police car blinks red lights and trails me until I pull over in disbelief. It is Officer Barr, the same Officer Barr who had stopped me in this exact spot, years before, after my divorce. And here he is again telling me I was speeding, but this time he also notices my inspection is three months overdue.

Waiting for him to do whatever cops issuing tickets do, I sit low in the car hoping no one driving by will recognize me or the mess my life has become. If my daughter could see me now she would roll her beautiful mascaraed eyes and bellow, "Mom, get a life."

Officer Barr taps on the window. He looks no different from when I saw him eight years ago.

"It behooves you to go to court," he says, handing me two tickets on four pieces of curled paper. And all I can think is: I need a break.

Eighteen months. Maybe I shouldn't leave home for another year or two. What do I say in court? What do I wear in court? Do I pull the cancer card? The "my-

143

daughter-just-died-of-cancer card?"

For two weeks I wail about the tickets. Friends warn me I will pay over a thousand dollars between the two fines and the surcharges. Frantically rummaging through my closet every other day, I finally pick out a rust-colored skirt and sweater for my day-in-court outfit.

On the morning I am to account for my deviant behavior, I settle myself into the wooden pew-like benches of the Ithaca City Court. I survey the scene to find a familiar face, to figure out where I fit in and if I am over or underdressed. A man in a black suit stands before the judge and is told to pay four dollars to a local food store with which he'd had some entanglement. A redheaded preteen squirms in his seat, nudging his father who wears khaki shorts and rubs his face every five minutes, looking nervously from side to side. A thin, pale woman is six months pregnant, out of work, and paying off hundreds of dollars of previous violations, five dollars at a time each month. The judge jokes with a young man in an orange jumpsuit who wears chains around his waist and wrists.

The judge is the one I feel the most kinship with. A neon pink shirt is barely concealed under her black robe. She looks like someone who would understand a fleeting loss of control, about being human and making mistakes.

144

But Judge Rossiter never gets to hear my story. I do not get to stand before her to plead my case. She suddenly leaves the courtroom and the city attorney approaches. He waves my papers at me, the papers which show how I diligently got my inspection taken care of the day after Officer Barr stopped me.

"I'll make you a deal," the attorney says.

"Uh, is that how it's done?" I ask doubtfully, wondering why no one else had been offered "a deal" and why the judge had gone without seeing me.

"I'm going to dismiss the ticket for the inspection and charge you fifty dollars for the speeding. That's the deal."

"This is legal?" I ask, looking around for witnesses and still praying I won't get charged the thousands of dollars my friends had predicted.

"You can wait and present your case to the judge, but she doesn't make deals. I make the deals," he says. It feels like a bribe. I have no evidence to show for the speeding and haven't yet figured out what to say to the judge about it. "And there's an eighty-dollar surcharge," he adds. But my mind is already made up.

"I'll take the deal," I say, rising, my skirt clinging to the backs of my legs.

As I leave the courthouse I pass people in suits, in uniforms, in tee shirts and jeans, and in rags. There are people in wheelchairs, in chains, in tears, in defiance.

Some are in dire straits. I walk by a hundred different stories. I'm out a hundred thirty dollars but I still have my house, my car, a bank account, my friends, my health, ...my son. It is the first time in four and a half years I can remember counting my blessings.

Gratitude would soon become the lifelong song of my days. This is how it began. In time, I would come to see even the loss of my daughter as a gift. I watch the world now like it has put on a new, jeweled dress and makeup. Life awes me each morning and every night, and all the blessed moments in between.

FIELD OF REALITY

Julius Beck

"One must still have chaos in oneself to be able to give birth to a dancing star."
~Fredrich Nietzsche

I will never forget a beautiful experience I had in the middle of a cornfield last summer.

If I could fully "take you" there, to this experience, I would. But this will have to do until a time machine is created. It's definitely a time I'd go back to if I had the chance.

I went for a walk around a field near my house. I was deep in thought with headphones on, looking down most of the way. I was thinking about all the moments in my life that had led to this moment, and began to make connections I had never made before. These epiphanies came one after another into my busy brain, and instead of thinking "I have to write this down" (er, well, type in my iphone...), I simply immersed myself in the moment, and like a bystander to my own thoughts, I let them come and go. Negative thoughts crept in occasionally, but I let them go, too.

My anxiousness began to dissipate as I gradually began to see things clearly. My senses became heightened, and suddenly I was noticing things I hadn't noticed before, even having walked this trail many times. The smallest things caught my attention - the blades of grass gently swaying by way of the wind, the silhouettes of the tall trees against the blue skies in the distance, and the stunningly vibrant colors of everything surrounding me. Everything was alive, and I felt connected to it. I was glowing with delight and felt an overwhelming urge to run, just like a kid at recess. I spontaneously sped toward the center of the field, having no real direction or reason for doing so.

I watched my feet as I sped faster than I've ever ran before, surprising myself with my own stamina. The fresh air propelled me forward and every time I inhaled, it was like I was taking a breath for the first time. I felt infinite, like I could run forever. I didn't feel alone, or defeated anymore, I didn't feel full of resistance or bombarded with the traffic of thoughts that seem to take my brain's attention most of the time. I felt free from struggle, pain, regret. By way of letting

148

go, I didn't feel like I was just living anymore...I felt alive.

I closed my eyes for a bit, running without a destination, and felt tears stream across my cheeks, the drops dried by the wind as soon as they arrived. I didn't know where I was going, but I was going to get there. I was struck with so much beauty that I knew that I had to still myself to fully take it in. I slowly twirled around more joyously than Julie Andrews did in *The Sound of Music*.

Like a child in wild anticipation, I sat myself down in the middle of this empty field to witness the beauty of the sun setting. As I made my way back to my car as it was getting dark, I looked back to see only a red sliver in the skyline. "The only constant thing is change. But the sun also rises." I began to say to myself phrases (no idea where they were coming from,) of this nature:

"You are no longer a fearful person in a chaotic world. You're a piece of divinity that is meant to shine. Let go and you will release the pain. Heal by running to it, not from it."

Some of these phrases twirling around in my mind struck me quite deeply, and resonated with what I needed to hear at the time. I was overcome with peace, love and intense gratitude.

I'd walked on that trail before, and have since, but it's never been quite the same. But that does not matter really, because that feeling will stay with me wherever I go. I will never forget the beautiful song that was playing in my headphones ("Welcome Home" by Radical Face), and I will never forget to remember to see the beauty that this world offers me, if I can only get out of my head, and out of my own way to see it, feel it, and believe it is there, always.

WHAT I NEED

Chantel Dudley

"Happiness is a butterfly, which when pursued, is always just beyond your grasp, but which, if you will sit down quietly, may alight upon you."
~Nathaniel Hawthorne

"Ms. Dudley, you have a tumor in your right breast."

I guess when I heard those words, I wasn't too surprised. Growing up across the street from the Dow Chemical plant always haunts my medical history.

The tumor was soon measured and the paperwork was drawn up. A few phone calls were made. An email here and a text there.

Lots of sleep is lost when you're worried about things that are out of your control. Lots of consideration is given to intravenous street drugs when someone drops the cancer bomb in your morning coffee.

So as I shuffled through the doors of an 'imaging center' this morning, I weighed my options. If it was less frowned upon, would I turn to meth or heroin, should I have cancer? Would it be acceptable? Would it be as awesome as the Hollywood stars say?

No, I couldn't do drugs. I could handle chemo. Maybe. Radiation? I doubt it. After years of reading medical records of dying patients, I couldn't imagine that I would make a good cancer patient. I'm not a hopeful person. And I'm a realist. An overreactor? Mostly. Religious? When needed.

"Ms. Dudley, we are ready for you. Please lay on the table and I will need your right arm above your head. Yes, that's great. Now relax your arm and breathe normally," said the nurse.

She was pregnant. Bad makeup. Long hair. I'm sure it took her two hours to blow dry. She put too much perfume on. God that shit stinks.

And with that, the gel and the CLACKS and the HUMMMZZ of the machine went to work.

The AC was cold and the light was low and fuzzy. The air was clean and light and smelled like alcohol wipes and hand sanitizer.

"Sara" was serious, but smiled. Studied the images and molested my tit with effortless movements and glides.

"God, I'm a shitty person," I think. "I've done a lot of horrible things. If I had cancer, maybe I deserved it." Who says that? I KNOW people with cancer and they don't deserve it. My dad has cancer. My other dad has cancer. Two of the best men I've ever met in my life have cancer. I couldn't do it. I'm a wimp. Cancer? Couldn't be possible. Not me.

"Ms. Dudley...I need to have the doctor take a look at this before I let you get dressed."

And with that said, her stool was spinning and she was gone. The screen was now empty and useless. No picture of a tumor. My last name hung out at the bottom of the screen. Waiting.

The ceiling tiles, all white, stared at me like they knew the answer. The floor was slick and far below.

Maybe I'll cross my arms. Nope. Uncross. Screen. Still empty. Machine. Still buzzing.

My heart was beating. Then pounding. Now banging inside of my chest. My purse across the room looked like a puppy that I dropped off at the pound. The leather was sagging across the chair and it waited too.

This is fine. I just need to calm down. I'm sure it's fine. I just need to think about something else. I need to think positive thoughts. People always tell me that. Ok. Positive. Hmmm. God, her perfume still stinks. Ok. Sorry. Positive. Why am I sweating? Poor Joan Rivers. I wish I could have dropped some F bombs with her. Why hasn't he emailed me back? I don't want to go to work. Shit. Oh. Positive. Ok. Hmmm. I have a baby now. Everyone says she's cute. Lots of Facebook likes. She wouldn't remember me if I died. How sad. That sucks. Oh. Positive. Ok. Here we go.

Closing my eyes should bring some relief. Deep breaths. I hear that helps.

Has it been ten minutes? Damn it. Why can't I just think of something positive? I wish I would have learned to meditate.

And like a long lost answered prayer, the country station on the little clock radio finally stopped talking traffic and started singing.

And it sang.

And I closed my eyes.

And my mind went back to a time where I waited for a Jeep to pull into the drive. I thought about a sandwich that made my life easier when it was hand-delivered on my sick day at home. I thought about some patios, some beers and an old Mexican man. I thought about earrings being thrown across a room. Vicodin. A couple. Or more. I thought about wild days of youth.

Stupidity and selfishness. Shameful relationships. I thought about all of the things they tell you not to do.

I remembered a good looking guy that I thought too much about.

And it was fun.

And the radio sang its song in the cold, clean room.

And I smiled.

I smiled. Eyes closed. Positive. Out of the negative came the positive. Out of what people told me was wrong, what we told ourselves was wrong, came the positive...years later.

I thought about nights. I thought about my high heels and his ball cap. I thought about how we always smiled. And it was wrong in its way.

But it was right. For then. And for today. It was right. It was positive.

"Ms. Dudley? The doctor says it's great. No growth. No concern. No reason to follow up."

And she was gone.

My purse was waiting and my bra and my shirt had missed me.

And I stood there.

I looked at my name on the screen. And I thought about all of the things I've done that have been so wrong. So bad. So vulgar. So misunderstood. I thought about how people looked down and how people looked away. I thought about my life and why it is what it is. I have no regrets. I have my life. And I live it.

I've lived my life the best way I can. By doing the wrong just as much as I do the right.

And as I walked to the door, and the final words of that country song played, I was thankful that my memories are still there. Waiting for their moment. To stand by my side. No matter how skewed or tarnished they may be to someone else.

And when I need them, all I have to do is think, "I need you. Now."

A DAIRY COW ON STEROIDS
Liwen Ho

"Distrust any enterprise that requires new clothes."
~*Henry David Thoreau*

"You look good!"

My friend's comment rang in my head as I stood at the bathroom vanity. The woman staring back at me did look good. As a matter of fact, she looked so unlike my usual appearance that I almost didn't recognize myself.

Only a few hours ago, I had woken up as an exhausted and grumpy stay-at-home-mom. Now, I had emerged from my cocoon as a vibrant butterfly. My black hair was curled, teased and pinned in an elegant updo. My face, once a blank canvas, had been painted in hues of pinks and browns. I wore a deep red gown and for once in my life, had some awesome accessories to fill out the top (an unexpected perk - pun intended -

of breastfeeding).

This is going to be a great day, I thought. I smiled like a teenage girl anticipating her first prom. In the mirror I saw a flicker of the old me light up my eyes. The part that had been dormant for the past year since my son was born. A year spent meeting the needs of a miniature human who depended on me every day and every night. I felt like a plum that had been sucked dry with nothing left save for a shriveled and wrinkled outer layer. Used up and spent.

It wasn't that I didn't want to be a mother. Or that I didn't enjoy having a child. I was the one who had nagged my husband for years into having children. Finally when he agreed to it, we conceived on our very first try. Giving birth had been fairly easy, too; after eleven hours of labor, twenty minutes of pushing, sans epidural, our son shot out of my body like a football into the midwife's fumbling arms. Since everything up to that point had been smooth sailing, I had no reason to believe anything after would be different. Wouldn't life be like those pictures in the parenting magazines of a blissful looking mom holding a sleeping baby in her arms? Little did I know how wrong I was.

I couldn't remember the last time I felt free to be alone, to consider my needs and wants. Since birth, my son had demanded to be nursed and held around the clock. He wouldn't have it for anyone else to take care of him, so I had been on the job non-stop. Which is why I stared at myself a little longer than usual in that bathroom mirror. I wanted to hold onto that illusion of independence that a makeover had given me, however brief it might be.

The day proceeded smoothly; the bride and groom exchanged vows, and the bridal party had a few hours of downtime before the evening banquet. I had planned to spend the time with my husband and son and sneak in some nursing, too. What I hadn't planned on was my son's reaction when he saw me.

First came the wide eyes. Then the screaming and tears. When I approached him, he cowered and hid his face, his chubby fingers gripping my husband's shoulder for dear life.

"Stop! He doesn't recognize you!" Hubby cried out.

What?! My son, whom I had spent nearly every waking (and sleeping) moment with for over a year, didn't know who I was? Two thoughts crossed my mind. First - Poor little guy! I just scared him! And second - YES!! I should dress up like this more often!

I couldn't believe my luck. I hid my growing smile as I left my husband to console our son. The day was getting better and better. I had already gotten glammed up and now I was officially being granted a kid-free day. No carrying, no diaper changing, and no nursing!

Wait, no nursing? I could already feel my

"accessories" filling up from half a day apart from my baby. There was still a whole evening ahead with dinner, as well as my speech in front of all the wedding guests. The last thing I wanted was to have a wardrobe malfunction should my boobs start outgrowing my dress!

Panic set in as I noticed two very distinct wet spots growing on my chest. I made up my mind. Without a pump (I hadn't thought I'd need to bring one!), I could only do one thing. I was going to manually express my milk.

I enlisted the help of my younger sister and headed to an empty room in the church. Another bridesmaid who needed to pump also came with us. She, the lucky girl, had an electric pumping machine and two bottles to work with. Me, I had two paper cups I found and two pairs of hands.

My friend called out from the other side of the room, "I don't think I've ever been that intimate with my sisters before."

I let out a loud groan and grimaced. "Hopefully she won't be traumatized after this!"

If there was a "Most Awesome Sister in the Whole Wide Universe" award, it would go to my sister. I thanked her for being my extra hands and moral support. She sat by patiently holding those two paper cups in front of me as I squeezed milk from my ever-growing boobs.

Drip, drip, drop, squirt. Drip, drip, drop, squirt. It was a slow, long and painful process. And hearing the efficient vrr-ing sound from my friend's electric pump did not help. Pretty soon she was done pumping, while I was still trying to squeeze the life out of my boobs. I so did not feel like the glamorous girl from that morning anymore. Instead, I felt like a dairy cow. A dairy cow on steroids.

The jingle from an old Chevy truck commercial played in my mind: Like a rock! That is precisely what my boobs felt like at that very moment. Two rocks. Two gigantic boulders that were on the verge of exploding.

After half a cup of expressed milk (both sides added together), I gave up on the "pumping" and put on my dress again. Thankfully, the wet spots had dried in the July heat and no one could tell I had just milked a cow.

Somehow I managed to make it through the rest of the evening. I made my speech, toasted the happy couple, and made a mad dash out of the restaurant. When I got home, I wiped off my makeup, undid my hair and took a long, hot shower. My son welcomed me this time with open arms and I nursed him for a good, long while. Eventually my rocks returned to their pre-"steroid" sizes and I let out a huge sigh of relief.

My adventure that day helped me see that getting

161

dressed up can be fun for a stay-at-home-mom now and then. But joy can also be found sitting at home in my oversized T-shirt, nursing my son and having him accept me just the way I am.

SPECIAL UGLY DUCKLING
Melisa Singh

"To love oneself is the beginning of a lifelong romance."
~Oscar Wilde

I wasn't a popular kid. My hair wasn't silky and blonde, but a jet-black, wavy mess that I'd wrangle into submission each morning before heading off to school. My high-water jeans were far from the cool Gap clothes the popular kids wore. I don't remember my parents having *conversations* during my childhood (they were much better at arguments.) I didn't know how to engage in chitchat and wondered what my classmates said when they spoke to one another, giddily playing in their cliques on the playground. What was there to talk about?

I was a daydreamer, constantly concocting fantasies in my head. Some about being born white and blonde and others about running away. Mostly they were about being wealthy enough to buy whatever my heart desired in the grocery store and moving to a different school where kids didn't gang up to shove me in the forest and stick pinecones down my pants. My mind was always in the clouds, my eyes always glazed over and my days filled with teachers or classmates abruptly clapping and snapping in front of my face: "Wake up!", "What are you staring at?", "Pay attention." Needless to say, I didn't fit in. And I certainly didn't feel special.

As I got older, my daydreams changed and I dreamed of finding the valiant prince who would make me feel like a princess. Years went by and this single fantasy kept me humming despite the continued bullying. In high school, I found acceptance in a small church, far enough away from my hometown that nobody knew me. I wasn't Melisa the weirdo there. I was Melisa - the poised, articulate Sunday school teacher. My pastor's son Christopher and I were two sparkling jewels in the eyes of our inner-city congregation. After a couple years of friendship we started dating and I believed I had found my prince charming.

I dreamed about the day when Christopher would take me to my prom.

Finally, the kids that I grew up with would see the real version of me. Beautiful, cleaned up and sparkling in a dress that showed the figure I usually hid behind a big sweatshirt.

They'd see that I had a boyfriend, a real boyfriend who was proud of me and would stand up for me should anyone be cruel. We would dance and smile and laugh. I would feel special.

The time arrived. Senior year. Prom was around the corner and I had already picked out my dress. A pretty, soft-pink A-frame gown with spaghetti straps, a cinched waist and two layers of tulle beneath the silk-cotton blend. To this day, I have never seen myself look so beautiful as the day I tried it on. I envisioned the one upcoming night where this dejected ugly duckling could finally be a swan.

Soon after, I was pulled into the pastor's office for a meeting. Christopher, his parents and I sat down and they told me that the prom just wasn't a good idea. It was bad enough that I went to a "secular" school, but the notion that I would want to writhe on the dance floor like a heathen with their son was simply unacceptable. "There is too much temptation," Pastor Moore said. I cried streams of unbroken tears that fell in puddles on my choir gown before finally catching my breath enough to beg them to change their minds. They asked Christopher what he wanted. He didn't seem to care. That was that.

Christopher's private Christian school had a "prom-alternative" at the end of the school year that we could attend instead. That was the plan. "That's just as good," I thought to myself. The day my high school held the senior prom I didn't want to be at home alone, so I decided to make it a fun evening and bring Christopher out for a night on the town. I had several things planned and even printed out an itinerary of our romantic date night. I had saved up to take him to dinner at the Grist Mill, the nicest local restaurant in my town. When we arrived, he looked at me strangely and asked why I picked that place. I just wanted it to be special.

A few weeks later, I asked Christopher to share details about his upcoming "prom-alternative" and he confessed to me that he already went. "What do you mean you went? Where was it? Who did you go with?" It was at the Grist Mill. He brought another girl. Someone in his school was feeling "down," and he said he felt bad for her. "You brought another girl? Did anything happen?" They kissed. We broke up. I was wrecked.

It took me more than a year to get over that relationship, but I finally did. In my first year out of high school, I began dating the one person in Bible College who didn't make me feel like an outcast for attending public school. Nathan was the smartest man I had ever met. He was nerdy in a good way, pushed me to think critically and *seemed* to adore me. So when he asked me to marry him after 6 months of being together, and despite the fact that I was only 19, I said yes.

I'd like to say it was because I believed he was "The One," but it wasn't. The truth is, I envisioned myself walking down the aisle, having my moment and feeling all eyes on me as I showed the world I was capable of getting a ring on my finger and a husband on my arm. I thought about the life we'd start together, proving the world wrong, showing everyone that I matter enough to belong to somebody.

As I walked down the aisle, I remember thinking of the phrase they say at weddings: "Speak now or forever hold your peace." Deep down, I was hoping at that point in the ceremony someone (my true prince charming) would yell out "STOP" and put an end to what I knew was a bad idea. But nobody did. I went through with the marriage despite my feelings, and ended up feeling disrespected and devalued. He was far from my prince charming. We finally ended things four (long) years later.

I thought divorce was going to be a badge of shame, but instead it was the beginning of a wonderful rebirth. Something changed in me. I recognized that I had the power to be who I wanted to be, live where I wanted to live and create a life that made me feel special. I moved to New York City and started a fresh life far from the bad memories of my past. Each day my confidence grew as I discovered who I really was and what I was capable of accomplishing. For the first time, I didn't fantasize about having a different life.

Ten years have passed and every day that I walk through the city, I feel honored to be a part of it - an atom in the blood of a beating heart belonging to the most wonderfully diverse, smart, creative, passionate being. My boyfriends have been princes, my adventures have been breathtaking and I have far overcome the self-doubt that dominated my early years. My special moments are many and now I recognize them even in the little things.

I was recently visiting family and had my four-year-old nephew, Dylan, on my lap. He's a curious little kid who's very attentive to visual details. I see him looking at me and I wonder what he's thinking. He pulls my face close to him in his chubby little hands. He takes his right hand and gently pets my hair. As he strokes it he says: "I wike your haya." I smile. He pulls his face back further, as if to see more of me. He opens his big eyes wide and says, "You're so preddy," with a bit of awe in his voice. My throat grips tightly, choking back a tear. And I have my princess moment.

Road to Knowledge

"No man's knowledge here can go beyond his experience."

– John Locke

MARKING MY OWN PATH: AN INNER CITY DREAMER
Mark Travis Rivera

"Perseverance is a great element of success. If you only knock long enough and loud enough at the gate, you are sure to wake up somebody."
~Henry Wadsworth Longfellow

Langston Hughes once asked, "What happens to a dream deferred?" Looking back at my childhood, my answer to him would be: the dream deferred sits idle like the neighborhood grandmother who waits on the porch to greet the children as they return home from school.

The dream deferred is a rose trying to make its way through the concrete crack on the ground, desperately attempting to bloom. It bounces off of walls like the stray bullets that took away a child's life long before he could even form a dream. It becomes the sparkle in the eye of the newborn baby so that its teenage mother doesn't have to lose all hope in her dreams. It becomes the rage of a people who still believe in Dr. King's dream but know it has yet to be fully realized.

For many young boys of color who grow up in inner cities, the "hood", "ghetto", or the "slums" as some would say, it's hard to see beyond the city limits and to believe in the power of dreams.

I am a Latino, raised in a single-mother household, living below the poverty threshold. I am a product of the public school system and a statistic we often hear about those who look like me. Regardless of the systematic oppression I have had to endure, I never lost hope. I knew from an early age that I would have to mark my own path — that if I wanted to pursue my dreams, I would have to do it my way.

As a kid growing up with cerebral palsy, I found comfort in writing in my journal. Being forced to sit on the sidelines as the other kids got to play left me yearning to belong to a different world. Writing was my escape. I have been writing poetry since the third grade and always knew I wanted to grow up to be a storyteller.

However, it wasn't until the death of my brother that I realized that life was too precious to let fear stop me from living as my authentic self. I was 14-years-old when my older brother Kamal was killed at the age of

22. For about a year I stopped writing. I stopped caring about school and felt overwhelmed by grief. Shortly after his death, I decided that I needed to live openly as a gay man. I was afraid of the backlash I would get from family and friends, but I knew that I did not want to waste time lying. The decision to "come out" or, as writer and scholar Darnell L. Moore puts it, "invite in" - was an act of liberation for me.

Coming out (or inviting in) and being comfortable to express my gender in a way that does not conform to the gender norms set by society allowed me to live the life I was created to live. The life of an artist and activist. We live in a culture that wants people to "be real" but not authentic, because to live life as your authentic self means to live outside the confines of other people's expectations and set norms.

I am the first person in my immediate family to graduate college. Despite the fact that no one in my immediate family finished high school, I understood that education was going to be the key to me breaking the cycle of dreams deferred.

Obviously, navigating higher education as a first generation college student is not an easy thing to do. I was fortunate to have people in my life that believed in my dreams and in me. They say it takes a village to raise a child, well I believe the same holds true for dreams, and it takes a village to nurture the dreamer and their dreams.

For a long time I struggled with guilt because I was trying to understand why I was able to make it out alive, while others in my hometown found themselves in the crossfire of bullets or victims of hate crimes because of their sexuality and gender identity. Yet I had the privilege of going to college, of speaking at schools like Harvard, New York University and other institutions of higher learning — sharing my story.

Now I am dedicated to helping others like me, youth of color from inner cities, LGBTQ youth, people with disabilities, and first generation college students. I want to inspire them to form their own path, to take the road less traveled, and to break the generational cycle of dreams deferred in their own lives. I am one inner city dreamer of the countless thousands of youth that imagine that there's more to life than what they see around them or in the media.

You see, marking my own path was not just something I did for myself, I wanted to show folks what is possible when they refuse to give up on their dreams.

In the words of John Lennon, "You may say I'm a dreamer but I'm not the only one."

A HIGH SCHOOL DROPOUT – WITH A MASTERS
Emma Louise Langham

"It's never too late to be what you might have been."
~George Eliot

I'd like to say it wasn't my fault I didn't graduate with my high school class. In 1956, the school system had a rule that married girls couldn't return to public school. Even though I planned to marry near the end of first semester my senior year, I confirmed with the principal that they wouldn't allow it and went ahead with my plans to marry anyway – so the decision was my own. I didn't even begin my senior year that fall.

We married in November. I was just seventeen, but my husband was twenty-five, had served four years in the Navy, and had a secure job. When I married, all the old biddies in town assured me - and my mother - that I would never finish high school. "Yes," they said, "everyone says they will finish later, but once they drop out, they never go back to school." They were wrong. I knew my own mind, and I was determined. My husband agreed that I could attend the Adult and Veterans' Division of Murphy High School in Mobile, Alabama, to earn my diploma. When I enrolled in my first class there, the instructor handed me a textbook and said, "Let me know when you're ready to take a test." That was the extent of instruction I got. No one taught anyone anything. If I chose to read comic books or nap during class, that was okay. It was my money paying for the class; I could waste it if I wanted to. But I really wanted my diploma, so I made the effort, learned the material in the text for each class, and finished my high school requirements - my entire senior year completed in night school.

I didn't want to participate in the graduation ceremony for that school, although I could have. These "classmates" were strangers, not the teenaged friends I shared my school years with. Besides, I had already had a wedding; I didn't need a graduation.

Despite graduating, I still felt uneducated...or inadequately educated. I'd attended my earlier high school years in a rural southern town; perhaps my teachers assumed that we students would grow up to raise children and potatoes, and needed little knowledge of literature and writing skills...I always felt that everyone else had read those classics of literature such as *War and Peace*, and that I was ignorant by comparison.

I had been married for twelve years and had three children when I decided to go to college. Like most women in those days, I had no job training or experience because I had spent those years being a wife and mother. I realized it was cheaper to learn to support myself than to buy insurance on my husband.

I was concerned because I knew I did not know how to write well. So I found an old textbook entitled *Writing with a Purpose*. I studied it all summer until I understood the principals of effective writing. In Junior College, an instructor told me that he had not written like that until he was in graduate school. My preparation had paid off.

Those first four years of college were so satisfying. Every morning I jumped eagerly out of bed, excited for the day. It was as though, after years of trying to cultivate a garden with a teaspoon, I had suddenly been given a tractor and plow. And after years of conversation with preschoolers, I was in a place where adults actually spoke and listened to one another.

College was a real pleasure, but not easy. Typical college life, with its parties and sororities, was not for me. I had three children in elementary school. I had a home and husband to care for. And as an English major, I had endless research papers and essays to write. I could not have excelled without my husband's help and support. He cooked meals and kept the children occupied so I could study and prepare assignments. It was years later that he told me that he figured, after I got my education, I would leave him for a more educated man!

I took my bachelor's degree in liberal arts, and then continued to get a master's degree in education. I taught high school English, literature and writing for twenty-six years.

I sometimes told my students, "I'm a high-school dropout – with a master's degree." It's never too late to complete your education. People drop in and out of school all their lives. You just have to make up your mind to do it.

HOW TO FEED A HORSE
Joy E. Burkart

"When I was a boy of fourteen, my father was so ignorant I could hardly stand to have the old man around. But when I got to be twenty-one, I was astonished at how much he had learned in seven years."
~Mark Twain

When I was younger, we had horses.

Well, we still have horses. But I cared about them more when I was younger. I cared about riding them, and being good at it. I cared about their sweet, solemn faces, and I cared about whether they cared about me. I cared immensely about being good enough at the family call-- a sort of whooping sound-- that brought them all to wherever we were, plodding happily across the fields at my grandmother's farm as they weaved between sleepy goats. It was always a bit magical to me, when I would stand next to my great grandmother and hear her make that call, to watch the horses appear from the other side of the hill or peel away from their grazing to gallop towards us.

There's something powerful and a little terrifying about having nineteen horses galloping happily right at you all at the same time. The first few times I hid behind whoever was making the call, but eventually I learned that they weren't going to hurt us. They were just so happy to see us.

On one day in particular, I cared about which way was the right way to feed a horse cantaloupe.

I was a very quiet kid. I mostly kept to myself and I listened to everything, especially what I was not supposed to. My father used to say that I had "selective hearing," because I would never hear him when he wanted me for something, but I'd always hear it when he assumed I wasn't listening and began discussing something with my grandmother that wasn't necessarily for my ears-- like whether I'd had too much ice cream, or whether the neighbor's kids were a good influence on me and my little sister.

So I listened, but I didn't always hear. It was my experience that adults could be right about things, sometimes, but in the end it was up to me. My internal logic ruled the day, that's what I thought. I was a smart kid: everyone told me so, and I knew it.

On this particular day with the cantaloupe, my grandmother and her boyfriend were teaching me how to feed a horse. You hold your hand flat, palm up, with whatever you want to feed the horse placed right in the center of your stretched hand so the horse can pluck it up with its big teeth and elastic lips that always made me giggle. It was obvious enough to me why you do this: so the horse won't bite your hand. But what I didn't understand was why my grandma's boyfriend would only feed them half a slice of the cantaloupe, and then throw the rest away. That seemed like a waste to me, so I asked him why he did this.

He looked at me, eyes twinkling in that Santa Claus way that eyes twinkle, and said, "It's too small now. The horses can't tell the difference between your hand and that piece of cantaloupe."

This seemed stupid to me.

They had just taught me this obviously foolproof method of feeding horses: palm flat, food held up and out. Of course the horse could tell the difference. Horses were super smart. Even *I* knew that.

Maybe I was intimidated by him-- he was a pretty silent guy, and everyone in the world was larger than me at that age (I was a smart, quiet kid, and I was also very easily scared)-- or maybe I didn't want to look stupid: I was smart and fiercely protective of continuing to appear that way. In any case, I didn't question him. Not to his face.

So, we fed the horses a few more cantaloupe, gave them a couple friendly pats-- I especially liked petting their soft noses-- and went in the house to start dinner. When my grandma wasn't watching, I slipped back outside and ran past her garden up the fence. I climbed the bottom two slats and held myself out over the railing to start whooping the horses over. Few of the horses ever responded to my calls; I don't know if it was because my voice was so high-- I could never make the calls from deep in my chest, like my mother, and my great grandmother could-- or because they didn't see me as a particular authority, but I didn't have much faith in being able to coax any my way. This time a few came up to me, which was quite the accomplishment at that point. I remember one of them was a horse I didn't like at all-- I think her name was Jazz. Jazz was temperamental, and I was never allowed to ride Jazz.

So Jazz trots up, and I'm thinking, "No problem. I'm not trying to be friends with her. I just want to feed her a cantaloupe." And I pick up one of the half eaten ones off the ground. I climb back up on the railing, and place the cantaloupe carefully on my palm. I'm next to Jazz at this point, leaning over the rail so my stomach presses into it, keeping myself in place; all in all, not an ideal position from which to feed a horse cantaloupe.

But I've got the technique right: what could possibly go wrong?

Lots, turns out.

Horses don't have much control over how delicately they eat food from your hands. Because their eyes are placed far apart on either sides of their heads, their noses and mouths are almost complete blind spots. All Jazz knew was that I was holding something out to her, something she was presumably supposed to eat. She couldn't tell which was my hand and which was the slice of cantaloupe, because it was now so small that it only covered my hand, and didn't curve upwards so she could pluck it up and into her mouth. It's not Jazz's fault she almost ate my hand.

I don't remember much after that. I remember a whole lot of pain-- more than I had yet experienced at that point in my life (that I was aware of, anyway)-- and I remember ending up at the sink in my grandmother's tan wood kitchen with her imploring me to open my palm so she could wash out the wound. I remember really not wanting to do that. People in my family were never very delicate with wounds, and I knew she was not about to just let the water wash over the palm of my hand and then deem it clean.

I remember looking at the half moon-shape indentions in my hand and realizing that the only way you get wounds like that is if the horse literally tries to eat your entire hand.

And that's how I learned why you only feed a horse half a slice of cantaloupe.

What lesson did you learn the hard way?

A LEAP OF FAITH
Chef Elle Simone

*"I am not afraid of storms, for I am learning
how to sail my ship."*
~Louisa May Alcott

On a cold December day in 2010, I took a leap of faith and uprooted my life. I packed my suitcase, withdrew my last $250 in the bank and took a train to New York City.

To make ends meet, I took a job running a women's shelter on the Lower East Side of Manhattan, while completing my culinary program. I was in class from 8 a.m. to 2 p.m. After class, I would hop on a bus, get to work and sleep in the changing room from 2:30 p.m. to 5:00 p.m. and start work at 5:30 until 1 a.m. This was my life. I studied at odd, early hours of the morning, after work, on my lunch breaks and the one day off I had a week. I struggled through this schedule, feeling my health deteriorate and both my work and studies suffer. Still, I didn't think I had any other options.

One day, I went to class and my chef instructor, who normally works by "the book," took the class session to have a very eye-opening conversation with us. She told us that we were in a critical stage in our lives where we would have to make some hard decisions that would require leaps of faith. I knew that that talk was meant for me, although I was still very afraid to make any extreme changes because it meant not knowing what was coming next. My corporate job was so much more comfortable and predictable than heading out on my own.

A week later, I collapsed in class and was immediately hospitalized due to exhaustion. I was overworking my body. I knew then for sure that I had to make some critical decisions about my career and myself.

I thought back to when I was a kid and spent most of my free time with my family at our "Central Station," better known as my Granny's house. We always congregated in the kitchen to help her make dinner. Those days were spent talking about our dreams, goals and aspirations. Granny would remind us that we may encounter struggles, but a life without risks is not a life worth living. That was the start of my love affair with cooking, and I knew I had to really go for my dream.

After two weeks, much prayer and counsel from my family, I left my job with the intention to become a real chef. After much searching, I found some small catering jobs. Though this meant financial struggle, I was determined to succeed.

About a month later, just as I thought I would no longer be able to sustain myself, I landed a job with an acclaimed Manhattan catering company run by a celebrity chef! I was the only female production cook in my division and I was really excited and grateful. I continued to cater independently and sell the cakes I made in my pastry arts class to the local barbershops and salons in my neighborhood. Shortly after, I accepted an internship at the Food Network, which ultimately launched my career as a Food Stylist and currently as a Culinary Producer. It's been 7 years since I took that journey and I love the career I now have.

Even with my success working with major TV networks and food magazines, I still encounter challenges - and I'm sure I always will. But I've learned to use the obstacles as lessons and strength builders instead of deterrents. Over the years, I've had rejections that have taught me to develop acceptance and know that everything is not meant for me and what is meant for me, will be...*as long as I keep taking tiny leaps of faith.*

My grandmother always said, "Nothing beats a failure but a try." I will live by those words forever.

CHASING THE AMERICAN DREAM
Leticia Rivera Davis

"Energy and persistence conquer all things."
~Benjamin Franklin

"Qué dijo él?...What did he say?" she asked. Before relaying the social worker's message to Mami's ears, I softened the words.

"Mami, he says that Papi has to look for a job right now or he'll stop the welfare payments."

My mother exclaimed, "Ay, bendito!" which is like saying "Oh my Gosh!"

My parents migrated to New York City during the Puerto Rican Exodus of the 1950s. With nothing more than a third grade education, they left behind their poor rural communities in the economically distressed island, for their dreams of a better life in the big city.

My siblings and I grew up poor and attended public

schools in the East New York section of Brooklyn. I do not ever recall my Spanish-speaking parents being overly concerned with my learning English or kindergarten preparedness. I guess they thought I'd eventually learn English once I entered school. They felt it was just as important for us to inherit their traditional values and home language.

Mami couldn't help me with my homework and Papi only got the burst of courage to speak English while drinking alcohol, but over time, I learned how to navigate between the English language in the academic world of "English Only" and the emotional and spiritual connections in my family's world of "Se Habla Español."

Just as I was fully versed in that dichotomy and in high school, my parents decided to move back to their island. Many Puerto Rican families uprooted their U.S. born children in the 1960s to live through the brief glory days of the warm, tropical island. While in New York, instead of falling into the bad neighborhood crowd, I had found opportunities to develop myself. I attended a Latino youth program that helped me envision education and success beyond high school. Even though we were leaving, I was more determined than ever to pursue my dreams and help my family through the challenges we faced.

I ended up being the first person in my family to

graduate high school and I felt so proud and successful. For my parents, having a high school diploma was enough, so when I expressed my desire to go to college to my parents, Papi grumpily advised me, "There's no money for books. You need to go to work after you graduate." His words cut into my soul like a machete cutting down a sugar cane stalk. *How could he deny my heart's desire?* I felt torn between my dreams and obeying my father. Pursuing higher education was unprecedented for a young woman in my family, and would be disappointingly beyond their means. I felt shame for what my parents lacked, and a sense of guilt for being selfish, but I decided I had to find a way.

I joined the military for 20 years of service and traveled the world while earning not only my bachelor's degree but also my Master's in Teaching. I'm grateful to my parents for raising us in the United States, where our ambition grew beyond those of previous generations. We achieved more than Mami and Papi ever imagined, and I'm proud of following my heart and chasing my own American Dream.

Family Ties

"After a good dinner one can forgive anybody, even one's own relations."

– Oscar Wilde

IT'S ALRIGHT TO CRY
Jenny Kanevsky

"There is a sacredness in tears. They are not the mark of weakness, but of power. They speak more eloquently than ten thousand tongues. They are the messengers of overwhelming grief, of deep contrition, and of unspeakable love."
~Washington Irving

A week before we were to leave for a twelve-day East Coast whirlwind trip, my younger son got sick. Not scary hospital sick, but he spiked a fever and for six days that damn fever hung on. His doctor wasn't concerned and said it was a virus, but I was worried. This fever just wouldn't quit. I didn't want to end up in an ER on our trip (or anywhere for that matter). He had just turned five and was a new kindergartner. Having him home meant I was on 100% of the time. When he's sick, it's 150%. Any mother will tell you.

My older son was eight and self-sufficient. Together, they've always acted like brothers. Sometimes they ignore each other and do their own thing, sometimes they play and giggle and have a blast and sometimes they fight. And the fighting. That's just a giant pain-in-the-ass despite being normal. When one is sick, it's worse. One wants to rest and have mom all to himself; the other is jealous but also bored. One wants popsicles and TV, the other wants to go out and play (*and* have popsicles and TV). There's conflict, tears, fatigue. It's a regular cluster - if you know what I mean.

I had planned to use that week to get ready for the trip and tackle a list of things ranging from going to Costco, to writing, to meeting with my editor, to laundry, to even spending a moment or two alone. To top it off, three days in, I caught the mystery virus. I pretty much catch everything; I have a weakened immune system due to a chronic illness. That is just my reality. But I cannot bring myself to stay out of my son's bed when he's sick with fever or needs cuddling. I'm his mom. That's also my reality.

I was feeling so lousy one afternoon. I was exhausted, sick and needing comfort, but encouraged that my son seemed to be on the mend. Wanting to capitalize on his energy, I had him sitting at the table, coloring, trying to get some actual food in him and take a break from the television. My older boy was doing well too; he was in his room Star Wars Lego-ing and having a great time. I was not faring so well. I felt like crap. I kept trying to reach my husband. He was going out that night to a concert and I wasn't going to ask him to cancel. Had it just been beers with a friend, I might have, but this was a special event. Even so, I needed to just whine a little, talk for a few minutes. I needed to hear him say "I'm sorry sweetie." I figured I'd cry a little, let it out, and then get through the rest of my day.

When I finally got him on the line, I burst into tears. I was so tired. It just all hit me. My kids have seen me cry before and react with concern and compassion, but what happened next was astounding and heartwarming and amazing. My five year old was sitting at the table. He jumped up from his coloring.

"Theo, Theo, come quick! We have to cheer up Mom!"

"Here I come Lucas! What's going on? Mom, Mom, sit down. C'mere, it's OK."

Meanwhile, I'm on the phone with my husband, but I am so overwhelmed by this I start crying even harder. I can't speak. They race to their rooms. One comes back with his blankie, the other a pillow.

"Here Mom, it's OK." Hugs all around, kisses, murmurs of support.

198

"It's OK Mom, you'll feel better soon."

"I know, Mom, it's hard to be sick."

My husband tells me he loves me. "Sounds like you're in good hands dear," he says. "Feel better." We sign off and my older son, Theo, guides me into his room.

"Mom," my wise then-eight year old says, "I'm going to play 'It's All Right To Cry' for you and let's just sit on my bed and listen to it. It will help Mom." And he puts in the CD of "Free To Be You And Me," music I listened to and loved at his age.

And I sit with him on his little twin bed, crying as he holds me and Rosey Grier sings:

> *It's alright to cry*
> *Crying gets the sad out of you*
> *It's alright to cry*
> *It might make you feel better.*

And I feel blessed and loved and, yes, I feel better.

THREE GIRLS
Lori Bogedin

"What a difference it makes to come home to a child!"
(or three!)
~Margaret Fuller

After our second whirlwind trip to Saratov, Russia, the adoption was final, and we had our three girls, complete with babushkas. They looked like angels. Anastasia, Alina, and Tatiana walked out of the orphanage that had been their home with angel wings…and into a Moscow hotel with new parents and no sign of their once shiny halos.

Over a decade ago my husband Jerry and I were young empty nesters when we decided to adopt. Our son Ryan, now an architect, was in his first year of college, and we were busy running our restaurant in rural Pennsylvania. Why would a hard working, middle-class couple that had just sent their only son off to college decide to adopt three preteen girls? The story begins with my sister and her family's decision to adopt Elaina. My little sister is always the activist, lovingly translated, the troublemaker.

My sister became involved with a project to bring a group of older children to the United States from the Saratov area of Russia. They fell in love with a sweet, nine-year-old girl named Elaina and decided to adopt her. Elaina, of course, had a friend...who knew two sisters...who all needed a family and...well, the rest is history.

Our history.

Alina was the first of the three girls we met. My sister and her family were devastated when Alina's adoptive family backed out at the last minute. Alina had little chance of finding a family before having to travel back to Russia. Enter Jerry and I. We met Alina briefly in a diner, where she promptly recited, "I Love America!" Two days later, she returned to the orphanage to wait and wonder. Her paperwork took two long years of heartache and determination. In the end, we gained not just one daughter, but three.

Our first attempt at communicating with the orphanage should have hinted at the challenges to come. In my first letter I intended to say, "Hello, I hope this finds you all in good health and spirits." I learned that what I said was: "Hello, I hope you are all healthy alcoholics."

For two years, we kept in contact with Alina through letters and videos. In each video we also saw Alina's housemates, two biological sisters, who were either actively participating or curiously observing. Anastasia was a year older than Alina, and Tatiana was nine. In our naively American hearts we decided, "Hey, why not? We'll adopt all three!"

We soon realized our three little blessings had a direct lineage to the last Czar of Russia or should I say - they sure thought they were royalty! The girls soon found that the only underprivileged Americans in the United States had adopted them.

It was a big transition, to say the least…and their expectations were equally big. At the orphanage, the girls were used to sharing everything, and "everything" amounted to very little. In America, they assumed that all young girls lived like royalty, or at least like the girls on reality TV shows: plenty of everything, apparently housekeepers, and especially no rules. With language barriers and cultural barriers—not to mention the natural chaos that comes with raising three preteen girls, let's just say we all had some adjusting to do.

When the girls first arrived, Anastasia was 13 going on 29. She was rebellious, opinionated, mad she couldn't date and annoyed that she didn't have a phone or car yet. She hated American food, American clothes, the American word "No" and, for awhile, her American parents. Anastasia is now 23, outgoing, strong and has grown into a beautiful woman with a kind heart. She is tough, smart, and can accomplish anything she sets out to achieve.

Of course, we all remember the challenges of those early days. Like teaching the girls they did have to do laundry, do chores, go to school and have to work to buy a car on their own someday. Above all, they learned the word "No!" This is the one English word they still have trouble comprehending, however now it is a good thing.

Those stories are not the stories we tell over and over at holidays and Sunday family breakfasts. Instead, we tell those quirky little memories that every family has—like the time Alina being convinced she had breast cancer almost caused an accident.

I was taking the girls back-to-school shopping, and suddenly thirteen-year-old Alina started having a fit in the back seat.

"Oh my GOD!" she screamed, we all jumped. "Tat, feel this!!"

"Yeah, it's a lump...so what?" said Tatiana, totally unconcerned.

"MOM...I...have...breast CANCER!" shrieked Alina.

I looked into the rearview mirror to see Tatiana shaking her head and rolling her eyes. Alina continued to scream, "Mom, I have breast cancer!"

"What's going on back there?" I shouted over Alina's nonstop hysterics.

"Tatiana, why are you feeling your sister's breast cancer? Alina, calm down and what's wrong?"

Tatiana explained dryly, "Mom, she has a lump." Then paused, "On her head."

I took a deep breath and said, "Alina, I can 100% guarantee you DO NOT have breast cancer…on your head."

Alina's response: "Oh…ok. Are we there yet?"

Alina is beautiful, smart, hardworking and our comic relief. She is funny and mature enough to be able to laugh at herself. She is a diamond in the rough and I hope she never changes.

Our youngest daughter Tatiana is sweet, exactly when she needs to be. We think she is plotting to take over the world. She is our beautiful, smart chameleon and can adjust to any situation in a second. She is a survivor - that is a fact!

Like the time everyone in Tatiana's science class got in trouble for cheating. The day after the test, the teacher announced, "The answers on these tests are all too similar. Everyone loses points for cheating."

"But Miss Teacher!" Tatiana protested. "I did NOT cheat!"

"I know, Tat," said her teacher. "Because you were the only person who failed."

Quickly, Tatiana asked, "So do I get extra points for being honest?"

We still laugh when we remember the time all three of the girls unknowingly used red permanent marker as lipstick because I wouldn't let them wear makeup and then it wouldn't come off. Or when the teacher asked where they were going on vacation, and they answered, "bitch!" instead of a "beach." And how they used to eat "sneakers" instead of Snickers.

The girls still tease their Pop over being the only one home each time one of them got their first period. I was in the hospital when Anastasia stood in front of Jerry—big tears in her eyes. Jerry just knew. He took her to the local pharmacy and the young girl working there helped get the things she needed. I was away on business for Alina and Tat's start, but by then Jerry was an old pro.

These memories bring tears to our eyes, but now they are tears of laughter. Recently, we all sat around and told adoption stories once again while Jerry cooked, and Avery, our grandson, ran around getting kisses. It was then I realized that these were not "adoption stories" anymore. They are a family's stories.

BOWLING WITH DAD

Jara Jones

*"It is not flesh and blood, but the heart
which makes us fathers and sons."*
~*Johann Schiller*

Hey.

So I'm talking to you, dad. It's lane four and I'm wearing rented, tight-pinching shoes.

I'm surrounded by actors. I love actors. One-on-one, intense, unyielding discussions over dinner. Watching them work. But put more than four of us together in a room and it's like a methadone clinic. Addicts being addicts. Loud, boorish choruses of our shadowed selves that can grate. Or, in my current situation, anxious, itchy, sullen types who grow paranoid based on the slightest unsettling stimuli.

Not judging.

I switch between these modes all the time.

And we're bowling. I always forget, until the moment I'm walking down a lane with nine pounds of sluggish stubbornness, why I don't bowl. Look at me. I'm 34. The most athletic thing I do these days is sidestep tourists on the sidewalk. But you tried your best when I was a kid, dad. Held my bony hand inside your weathered paw, offered a shy smile, reminded me to point my thumb and my wrist straight, follow through, pelvis out. It just didn't take, like all other sports. Naturally, I gave up and went back to my favorite activities: daydreaming about being in love, singing made up songs to myself, and reading.

It's the third frame. I've got a score of 6 at the moment. And you know me, dad. I'm not half-assing it. I don't half-ass anything. I'm taking my time, hearing your voice in my head, trying to follow the steps. And it just doesn't work. I'm eight again, and I have no skills and everyone else at this party is in love and happy and ripe with promise and I'm just a fat weird poor brown boy from Modesto who can't roll a ball straight.

First ball down the lane. I stare down the pins, and find myself pleading with you: C'mon, dad. Help me out here. Don't let me further embarrass you. Summon up some wind. Something. An earthquake, maybe. Just strike down these ten soldiers rising up against me.

And I roll.

The bowling ball shoots steady and fast down the middle for a few feet, then wildly skips to the right, lapping at the gutter.

Ten pins still stand.

My head drops. And then a friend spies me, she cheers me on.

Even though you died over seven months ago, dad, I can hear you sigh. It's an orchestral sigh.

You sigh because you know that this friend, with the holes in her stockings and a grin that shoulders a river of hurt, this girl is another silly crush of mine. Unobtainable. You sigh because you've seen it before and there's nothing you can do to save me from my foolishness. It's not my path, relationships and all.

While I wait for the ball to return to me, I apologize for my terrible bowling, mutter: "You know, I'm the only kid in my family who never won a bowling trophy".

I wedge my fingers into the misshapen holes, lift the mass, and walk down the lane again.

But just as I lean back to release the ball, she says:

I'll make you a trophy.

Dad, my wires crossed, and I almost sat down on the ground. I turned my head, choked back a sob, and disguised it as a laugh. Tossed the ball and knocked one pin down, head swimming.

Something like that shouldn't unravel me, Dad. I'm the same age you were with three kids. You dealt with floods and children who almost died and children who were mislabeled as autistic and incurable. I'm a potted plant.

I realize now that you were teaching me, even as an eight year old boy, that one's not perfect in everything. External rewards may not always be given, but instead, strength is to found in shared, vulnerable suffering and growth.

My role in improving this human experiment has been minimal at best. I need to give more people trophies. I need to stop wanting them so much from others. And if I'm given a trophy, I need to be grateful. Not glum out and wish it was bigger, or more prestigious, or a boyfriend trophy instead of a friendship trophy. Just give thanks.

I hope you're well, dad.

Love you...

THE TIME WE HAVE
Briana Mackey

"Time stays long enough for anyone who will use it."
~Leonardo da Vinci

Eighteen months ago, my Mom's oncologist told her that she had four months to live. He said there was nothing more he could do for her. He basically instructed her to go home and prepare to die.

The news came as a big shock to all of us. Six months before, when she was diagnosed with pancreatic cancer, we were devastated. But after surgery and treatment, we found ourselves at the beginning of 2012 with a stage 2 diagnosis and a lot of hope.

In just a couple of months, though, the cancer metastasized. It spread to her liver and her bones and was encroaching on her lungs. Stage 2 very quickly turned into a Stage 4 death sentence. My parents were beside themselves. As a family, we hardly knew what to do next.

My Mom decided she wasn't going to accept that she would be dying anytime soon. She most certainly wasn't going to accept living out her final months away from her three children and five grandchildren. My parents moved in with me - leaving their home in Idaho behind - and we sought out a new oncologist; one who dealt in hope. Mom started a "quality of life" treatment plan to keep the cancer from advancing while giving her more life and the chance to share quality time with the people she loves.

Eighteen months later, Mom is still with us. Though it seems her time is soon to pass, she's here and - except for the cancer part - we can look back on the past year and a half with tremendous gratitude. Mom has checked everything off her bucket list (she wanted to ride in a hot air balloon, hold a baby, take a family trip to Disneyland, and see shows on the Vegas Strip). My entire family has spent every significant occasion together (that had never been our practice before the diagnosis). I have run a marathon in my Mom's honor. We have produced huge greeting card and text campaigns to encourage and celebrate her. Just a couple of weeks ago, I threw a surprise party for my parents' 45th wedding anniversary. They renewed their vows. "Till death do us part" wasn't part of the ceremony. It didn't need to be. My parents have fulfilled their promises to one another. They will be together till the end of my Mom's life and beyond.

Over these past 18 months, I have fallen in love with my parents. We didn't have a very close relationship before. I had been incredibly independent and on my own for so long, but now I can't imagine my life without them (which is heartbreaking considering my Mom will die soon). I have fallen in love with my Mom's courage and my Dad's unconditional love for her. We have shared tender moments that have brought down the walls between us. We have said the hard things. And the things that would be hard to regret. I am at peace with letting her go. There isn't anything undone. There isn't anything unsaid.

I would love to tell you that all of this would have happened without the cancer diagnosis. That we would have woken up one day and realized how finite and fragile life is and readjusted our priorities to do all of the above. But, that's not the truth. The truth is that knowing my Mom has limited time left in this life has been a gift to us. And even though I know she has been scared and has had to suffer more than I can imagine, I'm sure there's a part of her that's so glad we have had these months and the knowledge that we had to make the most of them.

I think, if I had the choice between knowing and not knowing how much time I have left in this life, I'd choose to know. It would inspire me to live better. It would motivate me to love better.

The reality is, none of us knows how much time we have. Even the four month countdown delivered by Mom's first oncologist was incorrect. Only God knows the number of our days. And He has a plan for each of them. But despite that, I think we could all stand to live a little more like we're dying. Because then, maybe we would choose to fill our days with everything that's important - and spend less and less time doing what is not.

*Would you like to know how much time
you had left in this life or not?*

ABOUT OUR CONTRIBUTORS

Kevin Baker is a freelance writer based in Cape Town, South Africa. Besides writing poetry and assorted content for the internet, he roasts coffee, fixes computers and cars, and generally dabbles in all things adventurous. He is married to Helen, and they have three children.

Julius Beck is a 26-year-old Northwest-based singer-songwriter and nature enthusiast, living in a small cottage in the heart of wine country. She believes that by sharing our stories and inner dialogues, we direct our souls to a life of purpose, meaning and connection. Her greatest hope is that her storytelling, poetry, and music may reach and inspire others to recognize, acknowledge and honor their own inner artists.

Simon Beck is a nonfiction writer and blogger from Cincinnati, Ohio. Through her writing she hopes to give a different perspective on every-day life, while also giving her readers a reason to smile. You can read more of her work at:
www.coffeeandink1014.blogspot.com.

Sidney Bending is a retired graphic artist living on the west coast of Canada. Her award-winning poetry and flash fiction have been published in several literary magazines and anthologies. She is also a photographer.

Lori Bogedin is the author of the children's series Terrance A. Dragon and other stories. Lori is a full-time photographic hobbyist enjoying empty nesting with her husband in Northern Pennsylvania. Visit her website at www.loribogedin.com

Robin Botie is a blogger and Photo-shopper who believes she can design her way into or out of anything. She is becoming an expert in walking the tightrope between protecting her health and exercising her new mission to live life like it could end in an hour. Botie writes about finding joy after loss at: www.robinbotie.com/blog.

Joy E. Burkart is a student at New York University, majoring in English and History with a minor in Creative Writing and a minor in Computer Science. She aspires to work in publishing, and plans to continue writing her whole life. You can find more of her work at www.pbblyps.tumblr.com. Probably.

Anna Delamerced is grateful to God, her family, and friends. An aspiring physician-author, she loves listening to people's stories. She seeks to share with others about God's story of love, hope, joy, and redemption.

Chantel Dudley, a native Texan, loves to dose her audiences with grit and humor. Her charmingly haunting short stories and tell-all comic performances are blushingly raw. This up-and-coming artist scrapes out pieces of herself and unforgivingly serves them to you on a chipped plate she pulled straight out of your cupboard.

Shari Eberts has been practicing Bikram Yoga regularly since 2010 and it has changed her life! She became so inspired that she started a Bikram Yoga blog to discuss her experiences both on and off the mat. Visit her blog at www.hotoffthemat.com. She also tweets at @hotoffthemat.

Sarah Fader is the CEO and Founder of Stigma Fighters, a campaign platform that encourages individuals with mental illness to share their personal stories. She is an author and blogger, having been featured on Psychology Today, The Huffington Post, HuffPost Live, and Good Day New York. www.stigmafighters.com

Eileen Goddard is a New York City based blogger, jewelry designer, and vinyasa yoga teacher. You can learn more about her and her work at www.eileengoddard.com.

Carol Graham, an author and health coach, teaches and shares the art of becoming a survivor based on her own traumatic life experiences and her motto "Laughter is the best medicine." You can find more of her writing here www.batteredhope.blogspot.com.

Connie Gross is semi-retired after a long career teaching upgrading at the community college level. She still works part time in the area of adult literacy. In addition to digital storytelling, her hobbies include hiking, dragon boating, and curling. Although she is a passionate Canadian, she loves to travel, especially to the United States.

Judie Hathaway is a mother of two who have provided her with four grandchildren and four great-grandchildren. She graduated from CSUSM at age 63 with a BA in literature/writing studies. She has traveled throughout Western Europe and most of the US, gathering memories for her biography. Her hobbies include gardening and photography.

Liwen Ho is a writer and author of books for children and adults, in addition to being her kids' chauffeur. She loves makeovers of all kinds, especially those of the heart and mind, and blogs about her life as a recovering perfectionist at www.2square2behip.com.

Jara Jones is an actor, writer, playwright, singer/songwriter, and poet residing in New York City. In short, he's a well-spoken fool who peddles odes and nonsense. Find more of his work at www.21stcenturynonsense.blogspot.com.

Jenny Kanevsky is an Austin, Texas based blogger, author, and mother of two. She blogs at www.jennykanevsky.com & is a regular contributor at BLUNTmoms and The Good Men Project. Her novel *Chosen Quarry* is available on Kindle.

Clara Klein is a freelance writer in the American Southwest, writing about the life journey, philosophy and spirituality. She writes poems, prayers, essays and stories that she hopes will inspire others.

Mattea Kramer is a writer and professor who lives in Amherst, Massachusetts.

Emma Louise Langham is a native and resident of Fairhope, Alabama. She has published a slender book of poems, "Traces of my Life" and is currently writing her memoirs. She enjoys landscape gardening, music, friends and family.

Stephanie D. Lewis is a regular contributor to Huffington Post and pens a humor blog called "Once Upon Your Prime at www.thequotegal.wordpress.com. Her writing has also been featured on In The Powder Room, BLUNTmoms, Say It With a Bang, Better After 50, Midlife Blvd and Erma Bombeck Writer's Workshop. Her 2008 novel "Lullabies & Alibis" is available on Amazon. She is the mother of six and resides in San Diego, CA.

Kerri Lowe is a singer/songwriter, storyteller, and poet interested in the ways that telling our stories can help us heal. She believes that you can find your way out of anything through writing a song, or, at least, listening to the right one. You can find more of her work at www.kerrilowe.com.

Briana Mackey is a self-proclaimed "desert girl," living in Las Vegas and passionate about unearthing the stories of the people she meets. Briana has written personally and professionally for more than three decades and relishes any opportunity to journey through people's hearts. Follow her at www.wordywomanlasvegas.com.

Kaitlyn Maiani is mental health inspired writer that draws her attention to adolescent eating disorders. She has struggled herself but has found the hope in recovery and now wants to help those suffering from the same disease.

Bertram Allan Mullin writes with a goal of inspiring others. One of his works can be found with Bartleby Snopes: voted Story of the Month and featured in their biannual magazine. He also won the Exceptional Short Story Award with Writer's Ezine and Story of the Week here at StoryShelter. Find out more at: www.bamwrites.com

Traci O'Connell is a writer, educator and mother. She is a regularly contributing writer to *JLM Magazine*, a publication for people living with chronic illness and author of the blog *"Off the Top of My Head."* Check out her writing at tracioconnellwrites.wordpress.com & tracioconnellwrites.blogspot.com

Tex Parker, the Singing Cowboy, lives in La Grange, Texas and and travels the country as a comedian and musician. Find more of his fun stories and comedy video clips at www.texparker.com

Mark Travis Rivera is an award-winning activist, choreographer, dancer, and writer based in Northern New Jersey who shares stories about being Latino, gay, disabled, and femme. You can learn more about Mark by visiting www.MarkTravisRivera.com | @MarkTravRivera

Leticia Rivera Davis is a U.S. Army Retired Master Sergeant, experienced Spanish Teacher and aspiring memoir writer. Her poor upbringing in Brooklyn, New York and her valued family ties to Puerto Rico are topics for her journeys in the military, education and writing. If you'd like to connect with her, send email to letrausa.rivera@gmail.com.

Jim Ross is a recently retired health researcher who has published in several journals over the last three years, including *The Atlantic, Friends Journal, Pif Magazine, Up the Staircase, and Drunken Odyssey*, with forthcoming in *Dirty Chai, Lunch Ticket and Cactus Heart*. He and his wife passionately aspire to become grandparents of twins and to spend more time in Southern France.

Kathy Sechrist is a writer living on idyllic Whidbey Island, WA and is interested in the power of stories we tell ourselves and how they move us through our transitions in life. She is currently writing her memoir, short stories and essays. You can find more of her writing at www.kathysechrist.com.

Elle Simone is a Detroit native; a self proclaimed nomad that landed in Brooklyn in 2009. She has a thirst for all things cultural, abhors monotony and can be found eating anything from Kimchee to KFC. Food Stylist, Chef, Risk Taker and Philanthropist, Elle is a Spiritual Being having a Human experience.

Melisa Singh is the founder and CEO of StoryShelter.com. Melisa received her Masters in Integrating Marketing from NYU, where she first started working on the idea for StoryShelter. Melisa lives in Hell's Kitchen, New York where she works as an entrepreneur, inventor and marketing consultant.

Rabbi Rebecca W. Sirbu is the Director of Rabbis Without Borders at CLAL- The National Jewish Center for Learning and Leadership. She rabbis differently. Follow her on twitter @rabbirebecca and connect on www.rabbiswithoutborders.org.

John Vercher is a writer located in suburban Philadelphia. He is currently enrolled in the MFA in

Creative Writing Program at Southern New Hampshire University and is at work on his first novel.

Shannon Etheridge Whitten is a Nurse Practitioner by profession. She is a published poet, raconteur, short prose writer and nature photographer. She has published in the American Journal of Cardiology and writes for various medical journals. She has an upcoming book of short prose and poetry.

Jennifer Wolfe is a mom and middle school teacher who loves nothing more than watching kids be brave, courageous and navigate the world. Jennifer's stories and reflections appear regularly on her blog, mamawolfe, as well as on The Huffington Post, Bonbon Break, Mamapedia, Mamalode, Midlife Boulevard, Blogher, and Project Underblog. Connect with Jennifer on www.jenniferwolfe.net.

Liza D. Wolfe is a native Texan who fills her hours being her mom's full-time caregiver and raising two beautiful granddaughters. Reading, writing, and gardening are her therapies for life's little stresses.

Edie Wyatt writes about being a new lesbian in her 30s (and other things) on the New Lesbian blog (www.itsanewlesbian.blogspot.com). Her work has appeared on XOJane and in HerShe magazine. Edie's memoir about self-discovery, growing up, and the surprise of sexual fluidity, "Married, Divorced, and Gay by 30," will be published later this year.

Keri Yeagley is a NY mom, nurse, and writer. You can read more of her stories on StoryShelter. You can also visit www.GoFundMe.com/m9ijho where funds are being raised for Anaya's college education. Let's break the pattern.

Do you have a story you'd like to share?

Start writing on

www.StoryShelter.com.

You just might be selected for our next book!